MODERN DRUMMER® Legends

DANNY SERAPHINE

Modern Drummer Publisher / CEO - **David Frangioni**

Managing Director / SVP - **David Hakim**

Director of Content / Editor - **Mark Griffith**

Senior Art Director - **Scott Beinstock**

Layout and Design - **John Glozek, Jr.**

Music Transcription - **Terry Branam**

Editorial - **Michael Finkelstein**

Archivist - **Felipe Laverde**

Published by:
Modern Drummer Publications
1279 W Palmetto Park Rd
PO Box 276064
Boca Raton, FL 33427

Modern Drummer always strives for the best possible content available.
There may be some photos in this issue that do not meet our highest standards.
We have included them for their historical significance, rarity, and importance.
Danny was kind enough to share these photos with us, and we wanted to share them with you.

Subscribe to *Modern Drummer*: moderndummer.com/subscribe

For videos, visit and subscribe to the
"Modern Drummer Official" YouTube channel

- CONTENTS -

A NOTE FROM THE PUBLISHER

Danny Seraphine is a great drummer, an inspiration, and I'm proud to say, a friend.

I remember hearing Danny's drumming on vinyl LPs—and then 8-tracks (!)—with Chicago in the '70s, fusing jazz and rock in a way I had never heard done so masterfully. I had the privilege of seeing Danny perform live with Chicago several times, and every time was a lesson in musicality, taste, and chops. I was inspired to hear a rock drummer bring such finesse and creative fills to each song, while always driving the band hard. His identifiable sound—and his commitment to always serving the music perfectly with his drumming—is one of the reasons Chicago ascended to the forefront of pop/rock.

Here we are, decades later, and Danny's drumming is still in top form. In fact, I heard him play live recently, and his playing is better than ever. For all that he has brought to the art of drumming—and music in general—Danny has reached the status of legend. I'm very excited for you to experience the pages ahead in Danny Seraphine LEGENDS.

David Frangioni
CEO/Publisher of Modern Drummer Publications, Inc.

- INTRODUCTION -

Whether you choose to call Chicago's music rock, jazz, jazz-rock, rock-jazz, or fusion, it is music that is vitally important to the evolution of American music and rock and roll. And although he left the band in 1990, it was Danny Seraphine's musical vision that set the original version of the band CTA (now known as Chicago) on track to change the path of rock and roll. With the inclusion of a horn section, and the assimilation of everything from Varese' to Don Ellis's Big Band to The Rascals, Chicago altered the course of rock and roll. And at the center of it all was drumming LEGEND Danny Seraphine.

His drumming fused the swinging big band influences of Gene Krupa and Buddy Rich, with the elasticity and intensity of Tony Williams and Elvin Jones. He had the swing and swagger of Papa Jo Jones and Joe Dukes, and the musicality of Grady Tate and Shelly Manne. On the rock side of things Danny combined the rock drumming perfection of Hal Blaine and Earl Palmer, the perfectly crafted parts of Ringo, and the rock and roll swagger of Dino Danelli. If this sounds like an inordinate amount of musical influence to be found in just one drummer, listen to the music and read through the drumming transcriptions. It's all there! Then read Danny's brand new and extensive LEGENDS interview and all of his past features in this book. He details his musical evolution, the story of Chicago, and exactly what made Chicago's music so special.

For many drummers of a certain age, the love affair with the drums and rock and roll started with The Beatles and Ringo Starr on The Ed Sullivan Show. But for a slightly later generation of musicians, it was the intrigue and the audacity of the band Chicago. Was it jazz? Was it rock? What time signature is that? What are those horn players doing on stage with a rock band? (The band) Chicago puzzled, inspired, and excited musicians, all at the same time. But there was nothing puzzling about the music.

It all started with those highly crafted songs: "Saturday In the Park," "25 or 6 to 4," and "Make Me Smile" (and yes) "Introduction." The many different singers in the band gave us something to sing along with. The blazing guitars and soulful vocals of Terry Kath made us scream and howl. The rhythm section of Robert Lamm, Peter Cetera, and Danny Seraphine showed us where to tap our feet, and the horn section of James Pankow, Walt Parazaider, and Lee Loughlane blew us away with intricate parts that were more than just the horn stabs of traditional R&B.

Neither the band, nor Danny was an overnight success. Before forming Chicago, Seraphine slugged it out on the club scene. Eventually his hard work, dedication, and creativity was recognized, and success and fame came calling. But music always remained at the forefront of his mind. While he was enjoying the overwhelming success of a chart-topping band, Seraphine (and James William Guercio) guided the business from behind the scenes. All the while, Seraphine continued to study drums and music with some of the best teachers and musicians that music had to offer.

Like us all, his life and drumming career has had its ups and downs. But in a business that doesn't reward loyalty, Danny has remained loyal to the music he created. But that music has gone through changes as well. Seraphine's musical debut happened in the craziness of the 60's. He played on some magnificent music in the 70's (when less creative musical styles became popular.) He had BIG hits in the Big 80's, and enjoyed success into the 90's. The 2000's gave him the chance to revisit his roots and plant new seeds. Today, the drummers that he has inspired are some of the music industry's most respected and revered musicians.

Danny brings the wisdom of a well-deserved member of The Rock and Roll Hall of Fame, and a veteran of the music business. We can all learn from a musician that has truly been there and done that. Many of his drumming peers like John Bonham and Mitch Mitchell have passed on, but the music that Seraphine creates today with his new band California Transit Authority, is as important as ever. Danny Seraphine has matured and maybe even mellowed a bit. He lives a comfortably relaxed life and is very happy. However, Danny is still pushing the boundaries of rock drumming. He continues to infuse a sense of jazz musicianship and swing with his signature style of drumming, into the style of music that he helped create. Whatever you want to call it…

Danny Seraphine:
Musical Original, Drumming Pioneer, Hall of Famer

By Mark Griffith

When we talk about the beginning of fusion or jazz-rock music, we often talk about Miles Davis and bands like The Tony Williams Lifetime, Mahavishnu Orchestra, Return To Forever, Weather Report, and Herbie Hancock's Headhunters. A deeper dive will yield bands like the Free Spirits, The Brecker Brothers, Eleventh House, and Dreams. On the rock side, musicians such as Jimi Hendrix, Cream, Jeff Beck, even The Allman Brothers deserve to get strong mentions in contributing strongly towards the birth of jazz-rock music.

The drummers who first combined the jazz and rock approaches are all drumming royalty such as Tony Williams, Mitch Mitchell, Billy Cobham, Mike Clarke, and Lenny White. A deeper dive into fusion drumming gives us legendary drummers like Eric Gravatt, Narada Michael Walden, Bob Moses, Alphonse Mouzon, and Ndugu Chancler.

But for some reason Chicago (or as they were originally called, Chicago Transit Authority) doesn't get mentioned in the pantheon of jazz-rock's legendary bands, let alone given credit for their role in creating the approach. Nor does their co-founder and trail-blazing drummer Danny Seraphine. But Chicago and Seraphine, are jazz-rock royalty.

In 1967, Danny Seraphine's drumming was under the strong spell of Gene Krupa and Buddy Rich. However, he was playing around Chicago in R&B/Rock bands like Jimmy Ford and the Executives and The Missing Links. After being introduced to Bob Tilles (the head of percussion at DePaul University and renowned educator,) Seraphine, a largely self-taught drummer, began studying privately with Tilles at DePaul. That was when Seraphine approached guitarist Terry Kath and saxophonist Walt Parazaider with an idea.

Seraphine, Parazaider and Kath had the idea to put together an "all star" horn band of the best players in town and create a unique mix of rock and jazz. But this would not "just" be a rock band with a horn section like The Electric Flag had been doing. Seraphine's interest had been piqued by another band that used horns on their records called The Buckinghams; but he knew they (Seraphine, Parazaider and Kath) could put together a

I'm a very spontaneous person, and that's how I play. I don't like to plan things out; I like to live by the seat of my pants. I'm not saying my playing doesn't have any forethought, but I really just like to let it fly.

band that could do it even better than either The Electric Flag or The Buckinghams. Their goal was to assemble a rockin' horn band featuring intricate arrangements and magnificent songs being sung by world-class vocalists. Seraphine was confident that his unique fusion of jazz and rock drumming could drive a band like this and it's music into the stratosphere.

Seraphine, Kath, and Parazaider recruited organist Robert Lamm, trumpet player Lee Loughnane, trombonist James Pankow, and the six musicians became the band "The Big Thing." As they assembled the band, the musical influences would come from across the musical map. The band members all had very different musical interests: Don Ellis' Jazz Orchestra, Edgar Varese, jazz organist Jimmy Smith, Frank Zappa, Jimi Hendrix, The Beatles, and the jazz drumming of Buddy Rich and Gene Krupa. The Big Thing developed a reputation around town by playing original arrangements of cover song's, similar to what Vanilla Fudge was doing.

The Big Thing hadn't yet started performing their own compositions when they shattered the musical mold by adding bassist and singer Peter Cetera. Everything had fallen into place. Cetera, Lamm, and Kath all sang very well, Kath was a phenomenal rock guitarist, Lamm was already a budding composer, Kath, Lamm, Cetera and Seraphine were a formidable and flexible rhythm section that could do anything, an the horn section was gelling perfectly while playing Pankow's expert arrangements. The bands' musical vision was blossoming.

In 1968, The Big Thing drew the attention of musical visionary, manager, producer James William Guercio. He changed their name to Chicago Transit Authority, and the band moved to California. In California they opened for Jimi Hendrix, Frank Zappa, Janis Joplin and others. They soon became (simply) Chicago, and the world's most popular jazz rock band set a course of top 10 hits and platinum selling records that would land them in The Rock and Roll Hall of Fame in 2016.

Along the way there were tragedy's (guitarist Terry Kath died tragically,) musical disagreements, squabbles, and various personal issues involving just about every

DANNY SERA
(DRUMS)
His technique and style puts him
in a class of his own.
Copied but never equaled.

DANNY SERA
(DRUMS)
His technique and style puts him
in a class of his own.
Copied but never equaled.

DANNY SERA
(DRUMS)
His technique and style puts him
in a class of his own.
Copied but never equaled.

DANNY SERA
(DRUMS)
His technique and style puts him
in a class of his own.
Copied but never equaled.

DANNY SERA
(DRUMS)
His technique and style puts him
in a class of his own.
Copied but never equaled.

member of the band. Simply put, the brotherhood of Chicago went through the typical ups and downs that go on within most families. However, in 1990, Seraphine was inexplicably fired from his own band. To read the entire story of Danny Seraphine and the evolution of Chicago, I highly recommend reading his book, *Street Player: My Chicago Story*. And while it's a fantastic book, there is a good deal of stuff that he just didn't have enough pages to cover. That's where we focused our interview.

MD: I'm sure writing the book was very therapeutic, what was it like to write a book about your life in music?

Danny: What I liked (and didn't like) about the process of writing the book was that it made me take a hard look at myself. I was brutally honest about myself more so than I was about anyone else. It was a very cathartic look at my life, and while I didn't want to do any character assassination, I was honest and transparent about what happened with my fracture from the band.

Life is a learning process, and anyone who thinks that they have it all figured out is going to get knocked on their ass. The strange thing is that some of our mistakes are actually what people like about us. Your character flaws are part of your persona, and some people might really like your flaws. Those flaws become part of what drives you, and as you get older you learn how to recognize, manipulate, and regulate your flaws, and not let them manipulate you. I never had a drug problem, but I detail some other problems that I did (or do) have in the book.

I'm a very spontaneous person, and that's how I play. I don't like to plan things out; I like to live by the seat of my pants. I'm not saying my playing doesn't have any forethought, but I

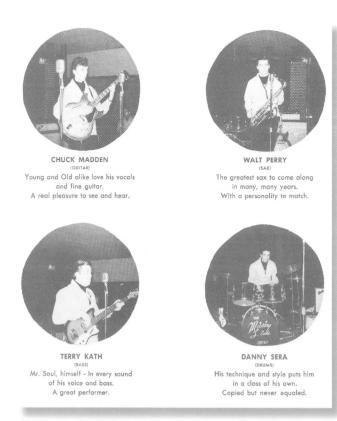

CHUCK MADDEN
(GUITAR)
Young and Old alike love his vocals and fine guitar.
A real pleasure to see and hear.

WALT PERRY
(SAX)
The greatest sax to come along in many, many years.
With a personality to match.

TERRY KATH
(BASS)
Mr. Soul, himself - In every sound of his voice and bass.
A great performer.

DANNY SERA
(DRUMS)
His technique and style puts him in a class of his own.
Copied but never equaled.

Band: The Missing Links

really just like to let it fly. I was very lucky, because on those first few records there was a lot of space where I could just go for it. I was constantly trying to integrate all of the jazz stuff that I was hearing from Buddy Rich, Papa Jo Jones, Elvin Jones, Tony Williams, and Gene Krupa into the band's music, and everybody supported that. As the band's music grew, my playing grew. I was naturally a pretty busy drummer, but I never planned on being THAT busy. We had a visionary producer in James William Guercio that encouraged me to play a lot. When we recorded "Beginnings" he was in the booth signaling me to play more fills, and (of course) I tried not to step on anyone, but he kept telling me to play even more and more fills. He had me do this because the drums were recorded in stereo, and my fills would literally cascade across the speakers as I played. I believe the first CTA album was one of the first records recorded that way. Like I said, I was very lucky. Most importantly, we all supported each other in any musical experimentation that we wanted to do.

MD: In your opinion, what is the difference between a rock band with horns, and a horn band like Chicago, Tower of Power, Earth, Wind & Fire and Blood Sweat and Tears?

Danny: In a "rock band with horns," the horns don't play lead or melodic lines, they play stabs and punches, and there's nothing wrong with that. But Chicago was horn band! There was a Canadian horn band called Lighthouse who were quite good, then there was The Buckinghams, and of course Blood Sweat and Tears. But I don't think any of those horn bands had the depth that we had. I think we had better songwriting, we had three great vocalists, James Pankow's groundbreaking

horn arrangements, and we also had an otherworldly guitarist in Terry Kath.

MD: If you look at the way jazz-rock and fusion developed. Chicago began in 1967. Miles Davis' "Filles De Killamanjaro" came out in 1968, "In A Silent Way" came out in 1969, and Bitches Brew wasn't until 1970. The first Tony Williams Lifetime record was released was in 1969. Those are recognized as the first jazz-rock recordings, and Chicago predated all them all. Not to take anything away from all of those musical geniuses, but you were actually fusing jazz and rock before any of those legendary recordings and bands. What made you think of first trying to fuse rock and jazz?

Danny: I started playing drums in horn bands around Chicago in 1963, when I met Walt and Terry, they were in a rock band with horns called Jimmy Ford and the Executives. The three of us developed a strong loyalty to each other, and ironically were all fired when The Executives merged with another horn band called The Mob. Then we formed The Missing Links; but there was really nothing unique about that band. So when The Missing Links ran it's course and were breaking up, Terry and Walt were about to go off on their own different lives and musical ways. I panicked, and approached Walt and said I don't want to stop playing with you guys, so let's give it one more shot. Let's put together an all-star band, we will get all the best cats in the city. At the time Terry was playing bass with both the Executives and The Missing Links, but he was a closet guitarist. Walt and I both knew he was a great guitarist, so we asked him to play guitar in our new all-star band.

MD: Was there anything musically that you were hearing at the time, that was pushing you in the direction of fusing rock and jazz?

Danny: I do remember hearing the Beatles record "Got To Get You Into My Life" and thinking, "Cool, the Beatles are using brass just like us!" That was a cool confirmation that we were on the right musical track. But that wasn't jazz-rock. Maybe more importantly, and no one ever really mentions this. Buddy Rich's band was playing some rock oriented music at that time and I really liked that, he actually had a nice rock feel. I really dug the way Buddy pushed his band, the musicality that he kicked those rock-ish tunes with, was amazing. Of course there was Buddy's soloing and the chops thing, but he never gets credit for how fantastic his feel was.

MD: I have always thought that Buddy's strong sense of groove gets overlooked.

Danny: I noticed this. The rock guys that tried to play jazz weren't playing it right. And the jazz guys who tried to play rock weren't doing it right. That isn't a criticism, it's a reality. I figured out that the pulse in rock was the quarter note, and the pulse in jazz is the swung eighth note. So instead of going back and forth between the two time feels, I tried to play them at the same time. By doing that, the two feels became seamless. I was consciously trying to fuse jazz and rock, it wasn't an accident, it was a conscious thought, that is what I was trying to do.

But in CTA/Chicago, I was in the perfect storm of music. Our rock stuff really had to rock hard, and our jazz stuff really had to swing. Then when we started to write in odd times, I really tried to make all the odd times feel like we were playing in four. I wanted to make them groove.

MD: When I used to play along with a lot of your tunes, the odd times were so smooth, and they went so perfectly with the melodic lines, that I didn't even realize they were odd times.

Danny: Cool, that's what I was going for. I was always looking for the spots to drop in a backbeat, because I'm a

We had a lot of talent in Chicago, and we were listening to everything. We had one of the greatest rock guitar players in Terry Kath, two of the greatest singers in Peter Cetera and Terry Kath, a great songwriter in Robert Lamm (who also sang really well.) James Pankow wrote and arranged fantastic horn lines. And because Peter is such a great singer, no one ever talks about Peter's amazing bass playing, but he really is a great bassist.

backbeat drummer. So whatever time signature we played in, I managed to put a backbeat in there. You have different patterns that you learn for each of the odd times, and if those patterns really flow, you can stop counting. But you still have to pay attention; you can never lose where one is! I don't like it when drummers have patterns worked out that make it hard to find the "one." I never did that; it seems really self-defeating. If someone couldn't find "one" when I was playing, they either weren't paying attention, or they were too involved in something else to even be able to find "two," "three," or "four."

> **"I don't have many regrets in life, but that's one of them. I never got a chance to hang with or get to know Krupa."**

MD: Did the odd time influence come from the Don Ellis band? They are another band that time has sort of forgotten.

Danny: Absolutely! When Terry wrote "Introduction" that was definitely Don Ellis influenced with the 19/8 sections. That is one of my favorite tunes. Don Ellis' band had a tune in 19/8 that we listened to a lot, and then Terry wrote "Introduction." Nobody played different time signatures like the guys in Don's band. The drummer's that Don had (Ralph Humphrey and Steve Bohannon) were amazing. Hearing them play really helped me play in those weird time signatures.
There was a tune called "Thunder and Lightning" that had a horn ensemble section in 5/4, and I played it like I was playing in four, just laying down the backbeats. But in every other bar the backbeat turns around.

MD: Vinnie Colaiuta and Simon Phillips use that approach a lot today on odd time tunes. Are there any Chicago tunes that are specific favorites of yours?

Danny: I have always loved "Poem For The People," it's got all of me in there. It has some classical stuff, some jazz, some rock, it's not a tune with a lot of soloing, it's just a nice tasteful tune. I like "Call on Me" because it has some nice rock-latin samba stuff in there. "Goodbye" is a tune that successfully merged real swing with a 7/4 Bossa Nova. I always liked playing the press roll and accenting the brass hits in "A Hit

by Varese." Like I said before "Beginnings" is probably my landmark track because of how Guercio was exhorting me to play more fills, and how the drums were recorded. I also like what the band and I did dynamically on that tune.
We had a lot of talent in Chicago, and we were listening to everything. We had one of the greatest rock guitar players in Terry Kath, two of the greatest singers in Peter Cetera and Terry Kath, a great songwriter in Robert Lamm (who also sang really well.) James Pankow wrote and arranged fantastic horn lines. And because Peter is such a great singer, no one ever talks about Peter's amazing bass playing, but he really is a great bassist. You listen to the bass lines on our first record, and listen to what he's singing. That record stretched him to the max, and he really delivered!
That was a time of truly excellent bands. You had Santana, Led Zeppelin, Blood Sweat & Tears, Crosby, Stills, and Nash; those were all terrific bands. I think that's one of the things that is missing today, great BANDS! There is a culture that develops in a band, sure there's fighting, I can't tell you how many times we would go in to record, and I would be pissed at Terry or Peter, and that would fuel my playing. But that friction inspires a creative culture that develops in a band, and that can't be replaced.

MD: When you first put the band together Robert was playing organ, which included playing bass lines on the pedals. You didn't have a bassist. Tony Williams did the same thing in Lifetime. Did you do that out of necessity, or was that a jazz influence?

Danny: That was a jazz Jimmy Smith influence for sure. But once we got Peter playing bass and singing, everything really took off.

MD: Tony did the same thing by adding Jack Bruce to Lifetime.

Danny: I hadn't thought about that.

MD: Can you tell me about the role of James William Guercio with the band? Was he a manager or was he a producer?

Danny: James Guercio was a visionary. He signed us to our first recording contract, he gave us our first name (CTA,) then he suggested that we change it to Chicago. He had the band start what was called a money purchase plan, which was essentially a pension plan. That meant that we all had something at the end of the day, and after 30 years or so, that equated to millions of dollars that we never would have had if not for his great idea.

Guercio was also musician, he was a very good bassist, and he played guitar. So he could make musical suggestions too. He was super intelligent and creative cat. When we were recording our first record, he had them mic my drums in true stereo. When I played a fill across my toms they went across the stereo spectrum. The entire drum set was panned as it was set up, ride slightly to one side, crash slightly to the other. James was a great producer. At the time when we started working together he had already produced The Buckinghams, and he did a great job producing that second Blood, Sweat, and Tears record.

That caused quite a stir within the band at the time, because BS&T were our New York competition, and James was producing them. But I'll tell you something, Bobby Colomby was an amazing drummer, they had an awesome horn section as well as a great singer in David Clayton Thomas and Dick Halligan wrote wonderful arrangements. Bobby's drumming, especially on that second album, is wonderful and just conceptually perfect. I didn't want to admit it at the time, which was just stupid. But you gotta give credit where credit is due, I really believe that. I know he's not playing much anymore, but Bobby's a great drummer.

That stupid youthful stuff also got between Bonham and me. We played some shows with Zeppelin, and he and I would just sort of sit backstage and look across the room at each other like a couple of gunslingers. It's a shame we did that, because in hindsight I think we really would have gotten along well, and really hit it off. I got along very well with all of the Brits.

MD: He and you each had strong jazz influences, and you have already mentioned some of your jazz influences, but let's go a little deeper.

Danny: I was all about Krupa and Buddy, they were front and center with me. If you listen to "I'm a Man" that is me stealing Krupa licks all over the place.

MD: Did you get to know Gene?

Danny: I don't have many regrets in life, but that's one of them. I never got a chance to hang with or get to know Krupa.

MD: Throughout the years you have mentioned the influence of Grady Tate a lot. You even call him a mentor, tell me about his influence?

Danny: Thanks for asking me about him, he was a special cat, and a fantastic drummer. My friend John Mulvey (who owned the Chicago Drum Shop) was very good friends with Grady. He told me that Grady really liked Chicago's first record, so John and his wife came to a gig of ours in New York and they brought Grady. I was honored.

I love Grady's playing on Jimmy Smith's record The Dynamic Duo; everything he played was just perfect. He is (to me) the ultimate musical drummer, and his time was incredible. Eventually we did a clinic together, and we did an ad for Remo together. He really pushed me to keep on doing what I was doing, and gave me a lot of cool musical and personal advice. Grady Tate was very important to me, both as a musician and a person. We often talked about how black and white people had to learn to live together and end the scourge of racism. We really celebrated the fact that blacks and whites had to find a way to get along, and wanted to show people how it should be done. I haven't forgotten our conversations about the need for racial harmony to this day. Grady was quite bit older than me and from the South, I could tell that there was a deep sadness in his heart regarding those issues. With me coming from Chicago, I knew what prejudice looked like too, but Grady and I were just trying to make the world a better place.

MD: Was Elvin a strong influence on your drumming?

Danny: Like so many cats, I went through an Elvin phase.

I just liked how he could float on top of everything. In my "Devil's Suite" solo I think you can hear some of his influence on me. Elvin could be really funky, I liked that. But Elvin was just a fun guy. He came to a Chicago show at Madison Square Garden, and I had him sitting side stage, and he was just amazed at the amount of people at the gig. He mentioned a few times that he wanted his band to open up for us. After our gig we went uptown together to see Buddy's big band play. Imagine that, hanging out with two of the greatest drummers of all time for an evening! It's was night I'll never forget.

MD: How about Tony?

Danny: Tony was more of a state of mind, intensity. I listened to the Miles stuff a lot; I really liked Tony's freedom, and (again) his intensity.

MD: I can hear some Tony in the "Devil's Suite" solo as well.

Danny: All of my jazz influences are in there; I can hear some Papa Jo too. That was my ode to all the jazz greats that I had learned from. Sometimes it was difficult to find the appropriate times to incorporate all of my drumming influences in Chicago's music. The Buddy and the Krupa influence's were pretty easy to incorporate into our music. I would sometimes even ask myself, "How would Buddy play this?" I really tried to play some of our songs in the way that I thought that Buddy would play them. But in "Devil's Suite" I finally got a chance to drop in some of my Elvin and Papa Jo Jones stuff too.

MD: When you wrote "Devil's Suite" how did you compose or arrange it?

Danny: Walt and I wrote that. We composed the framework, and I improvised the drumming and the solos within the arrangement. But I put a lot of thought into that before we recorded it.

MD: Let's discuss your rock influences. I'm sure Ringo was an influence, right?

Danny: I didn't get really into Ringo until later in my career, however I have always thought that "Come Together" and "Something" were great drum parts. I always had a real problem playing simply, lots of drummers do. But Ringo showed us all how simplicity could be beautiful. I love the way Ringo would just sit in the pocket and just groove without playing a fill. Later in the 80's when Chicago started playing less complex music, I really looked to Ringo's drumming for guidance. For me, Ringo's drumming was always more about style.
Dino Danelli was more of an influence by what he actually played. Early on, Dino's style was a reinforcement of what I was doing. He was a fan of Krupa and Sonny Payne, and he had a definite swing in his playing.

MD: Was Hal Blaine an influence?

Danny: Hal was a big influence. I love how he played on "MacArthur Park," and on Simon and Garfunkel's "The Boxer." The way he tuned his drums was so melodic, I really tried to do that as well. And his drum parts were always so tasteful. Like Papa Jo, Hal was a real philosopher too. But with Hal, you never knew if he was philosophizing or telling a joke. He was a hilarious guy. Hal played on some of The Buckinghams records, and I heard those a lot back in Chicago, because Guercio produced them. Their record Time & Charges is Guercio really trying to add his sense of musicianship and raise the bar. So (I think) he felt the need to add some session guys on the record. Hal was a really great guy, he deserved all the adulation and the love that he got late in his life. He helped create a lot of hit records for other people, he was a definitive influence on me.

Danny Seraphine and James William Guercio in the studio

MD: Was Hal why you started playing concert toms?

Danny: Yes, for sure. I have to also mention Earl Palmer as well. He was such a soulful and tasteful drummer, and a great guy too.

MD: How about Mitch Mitchell, you and him seemed to share some similar approaches?

Danny: We opened for Hendrix on a whole tour, so I got to see them every night, and they were amazing. Mitch Mitchell and I would talk about Shelly Manne, he was a big fan of Shelly's, and so was I. But Mitch and I were both bringing a sense of swing to rock music. I always admired the looseness of Mitch's time, his use of doubles, and the swing he brought to Hendrix's music.

MD: He could play that way in a trio with Hendrix, but in a bigger band you couldn't be that loose. I think if you played that loosely in Chicago it could have been a disaster.

Danny: I agree.

MD: I never got to see Hendrix, and you obviously saw them play a lot on the tour that you did together. I remember seeing the Monterey DVD concert for the first time and wondering if they were on that superhuman level every night, or if that was a case of catching lightning in a bottle?

Danny: That's what we all strive for, but sometimes in just doesn't happen. They didn't always get "there," but they were always reaching for it.

 Mitch and I had some similar "problems," I'll explain. There are old pictures of me playing while I was wearing headphones. I did that because there times when I just couldn't hear the band (or myself) well at all. Back then; lots of drummers had that same problem. But Mitch and I were playing similar styles that had some intricacy, which made it even worse. We both played traditional grip and with a decent amount of finesse. But I had this screaming horn section around me, and he surrounded by Marshall stacks. So we both dealt with the problem of just not being able to hear the rest of the band and ourselves at times. That's why I started wearing headphones on stage, so I could hear.

MD: You have had some very special teachers throughout your career. And I find it really cool that even after Chicago's success you kept studying, can I ask about some of your teachers?

Danny: Bob Tilles was my first teacher, he was a master educator. He was really charismatic teacher, he was always stressing professionalism and taste. I couldn't wait to get to my lesson every week. He played with the CBS Orchestra and Art Van Damme, but he stressed the importance of being a well-rounded drummer. He thought that it was very important to be able to play rock and roll, funk, jazz, and be able to play in a classical setting. He often stressed simplicity. He first taught me about traditional grip, and technique. Bob even let me use "trick sticking." But more than that he was instrumental in molding me into a true musician.

MD: I've never heard the term "trick sticking," what's that?

Danny: Using doubles, and mixing singles and doubles and not necessarily playing the correct sticking to properly turn the patterns around. When I was reading I would see rhythms written out with RLRL sticking's, but I would mix in various doubles while still playing the rhythms correctly. I don't know why I did it, but he thought it sounded good, and he never tried to break me of that. Those sticking's created a uniqueness that helped me create my own voice on the drums. Bob actually came out to see and hear me play one night. I was using those sticking's with the band in a rock context and he could really hear me trying to fuse jazz and rock in my playing, and he encouraged that. Although I'm dyslexic, he had me reading music really well. But whenever I read, I want to read from right to left. Under Bob's tutelage I went from being a good rock and funk drummer to being a true musician. Today I can hear other drummers play and I can tell that they are being strict with their use of sticking's, but that's what it sounds like, it sounds perfect. Some people say that perfect is the enemy of great. But we all strive for perfection, but I think you can be too perfect.

MD: When you moved to California, and the band started having some success, you began taking lessons with a legendary teacher, Chuck Flores. That is so cool.

Danny: Chuck was a great jazz drummer, and another excellent teacher. The reason I went to Chuck is that I wanted to develop my feet. I already had some jazz independence, but some of the bass drum patterns that I was playing with the band like in the song "Old Days" were really syncopated, and he helped me tighten that up and develop my feet. Chuck had written a good book on jazz independence that was like the Chapin book, but Chuck was a laid-back task-master.

MD: Later on you actually took some lessons with Papa Jo Jones right?

Danny: Papa Jo Jones was a disciplined teacher, a very

prideful man, and a real philosopher. Papa Jo had a wonderful presence and a strong sense of command about him. He was always talking about good posture; sit up straight, look at the audience when you play, stuff like that. He'd scold me and say "stop looking down, remember you're a showman too." Papa Jo was a terrific showman, but he really taught me how to swing. We did mostly brush beats and technique, and it was always about heavy swing with Papa Jo. That's an important thing because even in rock, swing is important. When you play a shuffle, that's a swing groove too. Although playing with brushes really lends it self to swing, I usually took those swinging brush grooves and turned them into rock brush patterns. But if you have weak technique it is really going to be exposed when you pick up a pair of brushes.

MD: Was he relating brushes to developing your touch?

Danny: Without a doubt, that was part of the importance of brushes, to help you develop your touch. He was such a masterful brush player, he really revolutionized the brushes. When we did our week of shows at Carnegie Hall, there was a night that Leonard Bernstein was going to come. Everyone was pretty nervous about the fact that Bernstein was coming to our show. But I knew that Papa Jo and his daughter were also coming to the show that same night, and THAT was what really made be nervous… Papa Jo was coming to our gig! Even more important than him coming to the gig was that after the gig he gave me that big smile and said, "You really sounded good tonight."

MD: It doesn't get any better than that!

Danny: Yeah, to get a compliment from Papa Jo or when Buddy complimented me on the Tonight Show calling me his favorite young drummer, those were two pinnacle moments. It was obvious that Buddy's influence was woven all throughout my playing, and I think he could hear that. That he could hear and respect what I was trying to do, that meant a lot.

MD: To keep things in semi-chronological order, I guess that I should ask you about your departure from the Chicago. You go into all of the details in the book, but I was wondering if even since writing the book, you have been able to reflect on that situation even more?

Danny: I'll try to be as constructive as possible. I was in a power position within the band; I really fought for what I thought was right and good for the band, that's all I ever did. But during the drugs and alcohol days that everybody (except me) had, I stepped on a lot of toes in order to keep things moving forward. Somebody had to, or the band would have fallen apart. A lot of the things that I did, I did behind the scenes. Our management knew, but I don't think the guys in the band even realized how much I did.

I was very instrumental in orchestrating the Chicago comeback in the 80's, I brought in David Foster, I brought Bill Champlin into the band, and I approached manager Irving Azoff and Howard Kaufman. Those three things were really important in our 80's comeback.

"James Guercio was a visionary. He signed us to our first recording contract, he gave us our first name (CTA,) then he suggested that we change it to Chicago. He had the band start what was called a money purchase plan, which was essentially a pension plan. That meant that we all had something at the end of the day, and after 30 years or so, that equated to millions of dollars that we never would have had if not for his great idea. Guercio was also musician, he was a very good bassist, and he played guitar. So he could make musical suggestions too. He was super intelligent and creative cat. When we were recording our first record, he had them mic my drums in true stereo. When I played a fill across my toms they went across the stereo spectrum."

When we did "25 o
I had the idea of pla
separate drum parts
loved the idea. So I p
the first part with alr
fills. And then I played
part with time and fills
can hear me answerin
with fills and crashes, I
the separate parts. The
the band thought we we
There are some little rub
final version, but it really
cool. You almost have to l
on headphones to really h
can hear the little five stro
are on a different set and s
During the solo you can hea
doubling the bell of the ride
and answering crashes with
crashes and fills.

There were a few things that I did that really alienated people, and that alienation led to my demise in the band, and if I look back, I might do a few little things differently. As I look back, it was probably time for me to leave the band, but it shouldn't have happened in the way that it did. No one benefitted from that entire debacle.

I wasn't the perfect drummer, or the perfect person. My vices were women and cars. But the guys in the band created and exaggerated major criticisms of my playing, and it killed my spirit. Unfortunately, the other people involved have been pretty good at re-writing the band's history.

The problem was that after the 80's comeback, I wanted to bring the band back to its original jazz-rock approach. Believe me, I didn't want to stop making hit records, but I wanted to return to a more jazz-rock approach. The newer guys in the band really didn't want to do that, and it escalated from there. Ironically, the guys who really pushed me out of the band (Jason Scheff and Bill Champlin) and I are now really close. And Peter Cetera and I are very close as well, but none of them are still in the band either.

dead horse forever, but I'm really happy and proud of all of the work that I did with Chicago.

MD: After that entire situation, I can see you needing to take a long break from music and drumming, I would have done the same thing. But when you decided to return, you studied with the other Papa Joe, Joe Porcaro.

Danny: After the traumatic experience and the betrayal of getting fired from my own band in 1990, my confidence was shot. I pretty much stopped playing at that point. If you hear someone say enough bad things about your playing, eventually you're going to believe them. So after 15 years of not playing, some people convinced me that I needed to come back and start playing again. However, I really didn't want to be like the athlete who should have stayed in retirement. I had a real fear of being that guy.

Joe Porcaro and I already had a pretty deep relationship, and more than anything I just wanted to know if I still had it. He convinced me that all the stuff that had been said

He was the first guy that really allowed me to have the drums sound exactly the way that I liked them. That meant wide open like a traditional jazz sound (except for a blanket or pillow in the kick,) and with only a little dampening on the snare for the backbeats.

What happened within the band needed to happen. My life had gotten off track, and I needed to rein it back. The biggest thing to me was the betrayal. The guys broke the bond that we had created when we originally formed the band. We had all agreed that no one would EVER get fired from the band.

I was a control freak, and I was really good at getting my way. But I have learned that you have to let things flow naturally, and when someone doesn't want to do something, you have to just let it go. I wasn't nasty about things, but I have a hard time taking no for an answer, and still do. Being a control freak only builds resentment, and destroys relationships. I had won too many battles, but I lost the war.

MD: All that I know, is that you were a co-founder of the band, and you got fired from the band, which sounds pretty wrong.

Danny: Yes but I had responsibility in the whole thing too. However, I had shown everyone in the band a lot of loyalty throughout the years. When people had personal problems, no one ever got pushed out of the band. I come from the streets of Chicago, and loyalty is everything!

Mike Mills (from R.E.M.) and I are good friends. He told me about how when R.E.M. thought that the band had sort of run it's course, they all agreed to just break up the band. I think that was really cool. Some people like the idea of beating the

about me by the guys in the band was just a bunch of noise; he listened to my time, and confirmed that there were no problems there. He helped me get my technique back, and we did some reading stuff. He was very instrumental in bringing me back.

As I look back on that period of not playing, I'm sort of glad that it happened. I'm sure it helped me preserve my body and soul, as well my mind. And I'm glad that I wasn't stuck on a tour bus for the last 30 years. I think that I'm a better person for it. But I was really happy to come back and put my new band called California Transit Authority together, and play at the Modern Drummer Festival in 2006.

MD: Did you ever record outside of Chicago (the band?)

Danny: The most notable one would be when I played on Maynard Ferguson's version of the theme from Rocky II. That was one of the most daunting tasks ever. After Maynard agreed to play a solo on our tune "Street Player" he asked me to return the favor and play on one of his tunes. His choice of tune turned out to be the Rocky II Theme (disco version), but he had already recorded it. At first he said he just wanted me to overdub a few fills and play a few backbeats. So after he finished his solo for us, we started to work on that tune. They played me the full orchestral take of the tune, and the engineer must have done something wrong while recording the drum track, something had to have malfunctioned, because the drum sound was horrible! Actually the whole track was a mess. In one section the strings were pushing, in another section the horns were dragging, it was a nightmare. So they had me play along with the track, and I immediately knew what they were doing… Maynard wanted me to redo the whole drum track. At that point I told them that it would probably be best if they didn't lose the original drum track. But they told me that they had already erased it.

At that point I knew it was going to be a long night. I tracked that tune from 7pm until 7am. I had to find the part of each section that was the closest to being in time, and split the difference between that and the rest of the band. I had to memorize where all of the band's time fluctuations were, and make the whole track work. Like I said, it was the toughest thing that I ever had to do musically. After we were done, Maynard gave me the biggest hug and told me that I had just saved his record.

MD: And saved him lots of money. What are your favorite Chicago records?

Danny: I like Chicago I, II, V, VII, XI, but they all have great moments and great tunes. What are your favorite Chicago records?

MD: I love the Live at Carnegie Hall record.

Danny: That was interesting because it didn't start well. At first we couldn't hear each other because Carnegie Hall isn't exactly designed for rock music. The first night was awful. The time was dragging because I couldn't hear my bass drum, the horns were overblowing, the singers were pushing too hard and were singing out of tune. Thankfully Terry really rescued that entire gig and recording.

MD: How so?

Danny: That gig was highly anticipated, highly advertised, and really hyped up. It was a sold out week at New York's Carnegie Hall. Then our producer decided to record it for a live record, so that added another layer of pressure. So after all of the problems and pressure that I just mentioned, things weren't going well. Until about half way through the second night we started "South California Purples" with a bluesy solo guitar thing. Terry just looked at me, and we started to play together, and then Peter and Robert joined in. We just jammed and we went through some of the most out and crazy stuff that we had ever played, it was a magic moment. And from that point on, we were razor sharp. Terry just really focused us, and we forgot about all of the technical issues and the pressure, and we just played.

That tune, and what Terry did, transformed the whole gig.

MD: Throughout your career, you have worked with some legendary producers: Phil Ramone, David Foster, Tom Dowd, and (of course) James William Guercio. Can you tell me about working with these guys?

Danny: Because the drums are the musical and sonic foundation of the records and the bands (especially in those days,) if you had a bad drum sound you would have a bad sounding record. So the producers really focused on the foundational parts of the record, and for us, the drum sound was a major part of that. Guercio was the perfect producer for the natural progression of the band. He would step in to resolve disagreements. He was more than a producer for the band, he had a strong hand in both our career and business management.

When we did "25 or 6 to 4" I had the idea of playing two separate drum parts, James loved the idea. So I played the first part with almost no fills. And then I played the next part with time and fills. You can hear me answering myself with fills and crashes, between the separate parts. The guys in the band thought we were crazy. There are some little rubs in the final version, but it really sounded cool. You almost have to listen to it on headphones to really hear it. You can hear the little five stroke rolls are on a different set and sound. During the solo you can hear me doubling the bell of the ride cymbal, and answering crashes with different crashes and fills.

MD: Was that the only tune that you did that?

Danny: I also did it on the end of "Feeling Stronger Every Day" and I did it on a shuffle on one of the later records.

MD: How about working with Phil Ramone?

Danny: He was the first guy that really allowed me to have the drums sound exactly the way that I liked them. That meant wide open like a traditional jazz sound (except for a blanket or pillow in the kick,) and with only a little dampening on the snare for the backbeats. When we did the TV show at the ranch and the seventh album, I remember that I had my black Slingerland set tuned to perfection. He came in and I asked him what he wanted me to do to them, (as far as dampening for the recording.) He said, leave them like they are, they sound great. He was the first guy to do that. He was an artist's producer almost to a fault. He would allow the artists to change things, even if they weren't as good after the change. He really went out of his way to keep the artist happy. We called him the painless dentist.

MD: What about David Foster?

Danny: Again he was perfect for the time period. By that time, the band had strayed far away from it's essence. There were drug and alcohol problems, and as a band we were just tired. David brought an added sense of discipline that we needed. The band had become a democracy, and we were "yes-ing ourselves into mediocrity."

MD: That's a great phrase.

Danny: Another one is, "Too many cooks spoil the soup." Unfortunately, our egos had gotten very over-blown; we were all "rock stars." The band had lost its way. Then David brought in session musicians, which I didn't agree with at all, obviously. He could have gotten great performances from the guys in the band, but he brought in "his guys." I really enjoyed working with David on the sixteenth album, we worked together like hand and glove; the seventeenth album was a completely different story, that was hell! But I don't blame him, he was trying to make a great record, and he had his proven methods. I even enjoyed working with David on the eighteenth album that was mostly programmed. We created some great records for those times, but I don't think he got the best out of me, and maybe he could have gotten a little more out of the band. I did enjoy working with him, he's a brilliant musician, producer and writer, and we're good friends now. I liked working with engineer Humberto Gaticia on those records, he got great tones and huge drum sounds.

MD: How about the legendary Tom Dowd, what was that like?

Danny: You listen to the records that he has made: Ray Charles, John Coltrane, Bee Gees, Aretha Franklin, the list goes on forever. Those record's all they speak for themselves. He's music royalty. However, when he worked with us, he was in a point in his life where he did not want to fight with seven guys in the studio. We overwhelmed him, so he basically said, "Look guys, go and make your own record." He wasn't the right producer for us at that time. But that was our fault.

A huge regret that I have is that George Martin wanted to produce us at one point. And our management convinced us to pass on him because they thought he was too old and we went with someone younger. I can only imagine what we could have done with George Martin. That would have been amazing!

MD: Is your new band CTA (California Transit Authority) still together? Those two records that you guys made are fantastic.

Danny: We haven't recorded for a while, but I love that band. Marc Bonilla is the best guitarist that I have played with since Terry Kath. He's a talented songwriter, arranger, he does everything; he's a great musician. The stuff he does with his own band called Dragon Choir is amazing, and the stuff he did with Keith Emerson is really good too. Keyboardist Ed Roth is world-class, actually everyone in the band is. Tony Grant is a terrific lead singer with a really soulful voice and such a wonderful guy. And Travis Davis is a great singing bassist too. We pick up different horn sections on the road, just because of the economics that traveling with a horn section would present, it's just easier that way. But after this pandemic is over, I can't wait to get back out there and see and meet people, and play music again.

MD: Any closing thoughts or lessons to share after looking back at your life while writing the book, and during our talk?

Danny: In this really great interview that we've done here, I hope that I have offered enough information to help and inspire the next generations of drummers in the same way that my predecessors and mentors have helped and inspired me. I'm always glad to hear drummers that I have influenced such as Gregg Bissonette, Todd Sucherman, Simon Phillips, Steve Smith, and David Garibaldi carrying the torch.

Lessons to share? Although this never happened to me, I have to say this. In my years in this business I have seen something happen a few times, and it always made me sad. I would like to warn the younger guys that when you are in the midst of success you tend to live larger that you should. You will have a tendency to want to live the image of the rock star, or live the image of the top session guy. Then when things slow down, and you're not the top band or THE guy, you wind up having to sell your house or your fancy car that maybe you shouldn't have gotten in the first place. I've seen that happen too many times.

MD: I think one of the big lessons of the pandemic and the shut down, is the importance of living within your means.

I've been influenced by so many amazing drummers...

Danny: But on the other side of things, you really have to appreciate the moment. We all have to realize the importance of what we are doing, and be aware of the legacy that we are leaving, and treat your own legacy with respect.

I would also be remiss if I didn't reiterate the advice to watch out for drugs and alcohol. I've seen the results up close with people around me. That has been the main curse on musicians, and nothing good ever comes from it.

As drummers, our job is more than keeping time. But the drums are where it all starts. Like Papa Jo taught, demand presence, and take command of what you are doing. If we are going to be responsible for the time, then we must take responsibility for the time, and own it! Our job is to make everyone around us sound better. If you live and play with that philosophy, you'll be successful. A great drummer can make a mediocre band sound great. Conversely, a mediocre drummer can make a great band sound (just) "ok."

Another tip for drummers; work on your lyric writing skills. Learning to express your self in a poetic fashion, and setting those words to a song, can be a blessing, musically and financially. That really saved me. A lot of my survival has depended on the lyrics that I wrote. And if I had learned to play piano, I would have been self-sufficient in my songwriting, but I never learned any piano.

MD: Did anyone ever advise you to learn some piano?

Danny: Bob Tilles suggested very strongly that I should learn to play the mallet instruments, which probably would have led to piano. But I told him that I couldn't do that because I felt that the time spent on mallets would have taken away from the time that I needed to develop into the great drummer that I wanted to be. I do have a little bit of regret because of that.

But I am really grateful for the life that I have had. I was a high school dropout from the streets of Chicago, and as a kid I was headed for trouble. Drums and music really saved my life. At the age of 15, I got an audition with Jimmy Ford and the Executives (with Terry and Walt) and after I got that gig, I never looked back. I have had a lot of help along the way, and I have a deep sense of pride in all of the music that I helped create. I am truly the luckiest guy in the world!!!

Danny Seraphine and
MD **Interviewer**
Mark Griffith

Hal Blaine

Gene Krupa

Buddy Rich

Mitch Mitchell

Joe Porcaro

Dino Danelli

Tony Williams

Elvin Jones

Chuck Flores

Grady Tate

Shelly Manne

Papa Jo Jones

Joe Dukes

Ringo Starr

Danny Seraphine
Equipment

By Mark Griffith

MD: You have played some pretty unique drum sets throughout the years; can I ask you about some of them?

Danny: As far as sound goes, I am (and have always been) a purist. In the beginning, James Guercio supported that, and I always appreciated that. Today, Don Lombardi and DW still support my purist views, and I am thankful to them for that too.

Let's start with cymbals; that's the easiest one to keep track of. I've been with Zildjian from day one. Armand and Lennie DiMuzio came and heard the band, and they signed me to my first endorsement, right there, and I have never looked back. There are other cymbal companies making really good stuff today, but I've always been a Zildjian guy. They're the gold standard, and so is John DeChristopher (onetime Zildjian artist representative, and drum industry legend.) For the first Chicago records I went the Buddy Rich route as far as rides, I used an all around 20" A ride with a nice ping. I also had a nice riveted Pang cymbal that I used on "Devil's Suite" and "A Hit by Varese." Today I am using the Avedis line; they really sound like my old A's to me. I really like the "Beautiful Baby" cymbal, and I love the Rezo Crashes.

MD: You also had a close relationship with Remo right?

Danny: Remo and I were very close. We developed the first Fiberskyn heads together. I was still using calf heads into the 70's, I just love they way that calf sounds, and I still do. But Remo said, "I can't have you using calf heads." So I told him that he was going to have to create a Mylar head that had the warmth of calf. So he said OK, and he started developing what would become the Fiberskyn's. He would bring me prototypes, and I would try them and give him feedback… We went back and forth with them for a while, until the first Fiberskyn's came out.

MD: I can't believe that you were still using calf when Chicago was touring!

Recording is one thing, but touring with calf?

Danny: Oh yeah, I used calf on the first two Chicago records, and I think on the third as well. That's when I started using Fiberskyn's, and I still do.

MD: Did you have all the typical inherent issues with calf when you were touring?

Danny: Sure. One of the reasons that my drums always sounded great was because I was tuning them constantly! I tuned my drums before and during shows and recording sessions, because they never stayed in tune. In colder outdoor shows I had them break a few

times, and under the lights they did completely de-tune more than a few times.

MD: Wow you are a purist! How about drum sets?

Danny: When it comes to drums. The coolest thing about the old (pre endorsement) days was that a lot of guys were using hybrid drum sets.

MD: Meaning different brands of drums on the same kit?

Danny: Yes, in the early days I put together a great set that had a Gretsch bass drum, Ludwig toms, and a Slingerland snare. Later on I discovered

Equipment

Danny's favorite and classic Rogers set, note the cannister throne

Danny's Slingerland kit

DW reproduction of the classic Rogers kit

Danny's first DW kit

Danny featured in Slingerland catalog

"As far as sound goes, I am (and have always been) a purist. In the beginning, James Guercio supported that, and I always appreciated that. Today, Don Lombardi and DW still support my purist views, and I am thankful to them for that too."

Danny at the Zildjian factory

Equipment

that Slingerland had the best sounding toms, so I put together a set with another Gretsch bass drum, Slingerland toms, and a Ludwig or Slingerland snare.

One of my favorite kits was a white marine pearl Rogers kit I had with a 24" bass drum, a 13" double-headed tom, 12" concert tom, 13" concert tom, and a 16" floor tom. I absolutely loved that kit, it recorded really well. I used it on the first two Chicago records. DW made me an exact replica of that kit, that's the kit that I played at the Rock and Roll Hall of Fame induction concert.

MD: I've seen that kit; it's a strange set-up.

Danny: I really like to keep my ride lower, like how Buddy had his; I did all sorts of weird stuff with toms in order to have the ride in the right place for me. On the third Chicago record I just started using my Slingerland kit with one mounted tom and two floor toms. There is a famous picture of me with that Slingerland copper colored wrapped set that is a mounted 13", with 14" and 16" floor toms, and a 22" bass drum.

I also had a natural Gretsch kit with a 20" kick 10", 12", 14", 16". I used that set on the third record too. Later on, Slingerland made me a little jazz kit

with a 20" bass drum that sounded fantastic. That was a black kit, and was Slingerland's version of my Gretsch kit. I went to 20" bass drums for a while because for rock you could play a little lighter on them, and they still sounded big and punchy. I still like 18" and 20" bass drum's.

MD: Then you went to what (I think) many people consider to be your classic set. The white Slingerlands with the Hal Blaine influenced concert toms, what can you tell me about those?

Danny: Those white Slingerlands were 8", 10", 12", 14", 16" concert toms, and a 16" floor tom. Like you said, Hal Blaine. Today, I think DW is making the best drums on the planet. I might be a little

biased because they are like family to me. But I sincerely think that Don Lombardi recalibrated the bar, and then raised the bar when it comes to making drums. That Rogers replica set that they made me (for the Rock n Roll Hall of fame induction performance with Chicago) is amazing.

MD: Now that DW has bought the Slingerland name and design, are you going to be doing anything special with them and the new Slingerland drums?

Danny: I hope so! I'm their Slingerland guy. Right now I am playing a white crystal DW set with a 10" and a 12" on a separate stand off to the left, and 14" and 16" floor toms. The bass drum is a 14" x 24", I like the shallower bass drums. The DW wood True Sonic sounds just like the older Dyna-Sonic, but they are easier to tune.

MD: Perfect segue way… how about snares?

Danny: Early on, almost always Slingerland or Ludwig snares, I was never really thrilled with the older Gretsch snares. But Radio King and Black Beauty snares are just hard to beat.

MD: Are we talking about the 1920's

This is an example of the hybrid drumsets that Danny refers to, note the Ludwig Bass Drum, the 5 lug Gretsch 12" Tom, the chrome knobs for the double mufflers on the top and bottom of the Gretsch floor tom, and the Rogers Hardware

Black Beauty's or the newer ones? And are we talking about of those 7" deep Radio King snares like Krupa used?

Danny: I'm talking about the newer 70's Black Beauty's. But I do have a gorgeous really old Super Sensitive, but I can't use it because it gets knocked out of whack really easy. With the Radio King snares, mine was a 5" like Buddy had. But I know the ones that you are talking about.

I also love the Rogers Dyna-Sonic; I used a wood Dyna-Sonic on the first two Chicago records. That drum was a little tough to get sounding good for rock, but once we got it dialed in and sounding good, that was a great drum.

However, right before we recorded "Make Me Smile" I went into Frank Ippolito's drum shop and he showed me a new Rogers piccolo snare that sounded so good that I bought it and brought it right to the studio. That's the snare on "Make Me Smile." I think I actually used that on a lot of that album.

MD: In the 80's you used the deep Valley Custom Snares on the David Foster produced records. Do you remember the dimensions or the specs of that drum?

Danny: No but I still have it somewhere. I do remember that Humberto Gaticia and I tuned it super low, and it sounded huge.

I should also say that I have always used Ludwig Speed King bass drum pedals. I just love the way that they feel.

LOOKIN

1979: The Rhythm of Chicago

By Robyn Flans

"I loved to watch my uncle who was a drummer, when I was young, but he only played weekends because in those days, most of them didn't really devote their lives to it. It was such a long-shot," says Danny Seraphine, drummer for Chicago, whose innovative sound first stirred the public well over a decade ago.Still somewhat of a longshot, Seraphine has managed to devote his life to music, and has become one of the most influential drummers of his time.

Seated at the poolside patio of his Tudor style home, equipped with a small 8-track studio, Seraphine looked the picture of California, complete with shorts and golf visor hat, as he sipped his iced tea and seemed to enjoy the interview.

Seraphine began drum lessons at the age of nine on a Slingerland set. He studied at the neighborhood music school in Chicago. He spent two years with one of the better instructors, but when that teacher left the school, Seraphine was disappointed with his replacement and departed. For about five years, Seraphine remained content teaching himself and felt he had

become a substantial rock, funk and r&b player, but finally realized that in order to progress, he would need to find a new teacher.

It was about that time when he met up with Walter Parazaider and Terry Kath. Parazaider recommended the head of percussion, Bob Tilles, at De Paul University, where Parazaider

After the move to California, Seraphine obtained the name of teacher, Chuck Flores, "who really helped me a lot.

himself, attended. Seraphine, only 15, and not having completed school, was not eligible for enrollment at the university, but was elated when Tilles, after hearing him play, agreed to take him on privately.

"He was really the turning point in my playing," Seraphine recalls. "At that point, I had studied a bit, but with no one as proficient. I was more or less a good, self-taught rock and roll drummer. But as far as stretching

out and taking it further, I had a hard time because my knowledge of the instrument technically, was limited. It broadened my scope in all kinds of music, as far as reading, knowledge of other forms of music, how to approach them and just understanding. I needed direction and he gave it to me, along with a lot of confidence. He said I was better than any of his students because I had the combination of the ears and I could read, so I was developing a thing where I had a balance of a really good technique and feel, whereas most of the guys had no feel and all technique."

For two and a half years, Seraphine studied with Tilles, while playing with Parazaider and Kath in a horn band called Jimmy Ford and The Executives. "In those days, all a good musician could do was back up single artists like Lou Christy. We played sock-hops and stuff like that, while we were also Dick Clark's road band to back artists, which was a great experience."

Having started out a "jazz fanatic," Seraphine's very first influence was Gene Krupa, soon followed by Buddy Rich. "There aren't enough great things I can say about Buddy Rich. He was a

G BACK

tremendous influence on me and always has been, and even still is," he adds. "When I need to look back to what I used to be and what got me there, that's where I go." Seraphine relates that one of his all time career highlights was when Rich told him he thought Seraphine was a great drummer.

"Then I started to get into guys like Tony Williams and it turned my head around because Tony Williams was a jazz cat who played like a rock cat. To me, he was an extension of Max Roach, who I also listened to a lot. Max Roach is an extension of Jo Jones.

"I never really got to play be-bop like I should have or sit in with big bands. I never really had the time, because once Chicago got together, everybody was totally devoted to the band."

Chicago actually originated from Seraphine's meeting with Walter Parazaider and Terry Kath at the try-outs for Jimmy Ford and The Executives. When the band eventually split up, threequarters of its members went on to become LeMob, a horn band out of

Chicago, while Danny, Terry and Walt went on to form a band called The Missing Links with additional members. "Terry was playing bass at that time, Walt was playing sax and I was playing drums. It was a rock and roll band.

When that band started to fall apart, Terry was going to go to Los Angeles and Walt was about to get his bachelors degree and was planning on teaching. He was thinking about getting out of

the performing end, so I kind of talked him into giving it another shot. It didn't really take much," Seraphine recalls, laughing. "So we decided to put together a band of tremendous players and talked Terry into staying and playing guitar. Walt knew Jimmy Pankow (trombone) and we'd already been friends with Lee (Loughnane, trumpet) who was in another band. They joined up and we heard about this keyboard player on the Southside, who was going by the name of Bobby Charles at the time. His real name was Bobby Lamm, and we got him to join up." By the time Peter Cetera (bass) joined up, the group called itself The Big Thing, until they journeyed to Los Angeles in 1968 and manager/ producer James Guercio renamed them Chicago Transit Authority, which was later shortened, when the real CTA threatened to sue.

Just last year, Chicago changed its producer to Phil Ramone and its management to Jeff Wald, and since its inception, over 12 years ago, Chicago has only undergone two personnel changes. One came about in 1975 with the addition of percussionist Laudir de Oliveira, and the other was imposed upon the group in January, 1978, with the tragic death of Terry Kath, who accidentally killed himself while toying with a gun. For the close-knit group, it was a difficult adjust ment to make, but Donny Dacus was eventually added on guitar and vocals and his first album with Chicago, Hot Streets, followed suit of the previous 11, gaining platinum status.

Seraphine feels extremely fortunate that he was always given the freedom to "stretch out and experiment" by the other group members. "I think because I was fortunate enough to be able to lay it down on record, I was part of an evolution where rock drummers were really able to take it a few steps further than it was and bring in other influences. I think Bobby Colomby of Blood, Sweat & Tears and I were among the first to really do that."

After the move to California, Seraphine obtained the name of teacher, Chuck Flores, "who really helped me a lot. At that point, I had a lot of technical knowledge and I was just looking for avenues for utilizing it as far as rock drumming. Chuck really had a beat right into where I was headed and the direction I wanted, which was incorporating the technical jazz thing into rock. He really helped to bring the two worlds together for me. He gave me a lot of bass drum exercises to develop my foot because the bass drum is so important in rock and roll, much more important than in jazz, but has since become incorporated." Seraphine remains grateful for the continuous educational experiences Chicago has afforded him. "I remember when we were doing our fifth album, we were in New York for about two months and I was able to take brush lessons from Jo Jones. To put into words what I learned from him would be a little rough. What a totally different

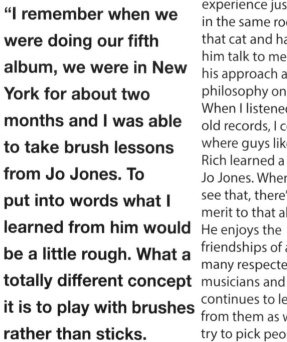

concept it is to play with brushes rather than sticks. I had used them before, but never like that. He pulled out some of his old records and I was amazed at what he could do with brushes. It still has helped me because when I pick up a set of brushes, I don't feel lost. I feel pretty proficient. Though Chicago never played the kind of music where I could get the most out of it, it was still a great education. He taught me a lot of little things, like posture when I play and things like that. It was a great experience just sitting in the same room with that cat and having him talk to me about his approach and philosophy on music. When I listened to his old records, I could see where guys like Buddy Rich learned a lot from Jo Jones. When you see that, there's a lot of merit to that alone."

He enjoys the friendships of a great many respected musicians and continues to learn from them as well. "I try to pick people's brains," Seraphine reveals. "Not for licks, but for philosophy, because that helps me more than anything."

Seraphine has adopted much of what he considers to be Elvin Jones' philosophy. "A good musician should be able to play everything, to really be able to express himself. But always a good musician must compliment whatever is going on around him and always

"I remember when we were doing our fifth album, we were in New York for about two months and I was able to take brush lessons from Jo Jones. To put into words what I learned from him would be a little rough. What a totally different concept it is to play with brushes rather than sticks.

keep his ears open. My objective was to play any kind of music put in front of me as good as it could be played, and to compliment the music, while at the same time express myself. My favorite thing is that I really just love to play a good drum part."

He often emphasizes the intangible qualities over the more learned technical points, often using the word "sensitivity" when describing his priorities. "A good drummer to me is a combination of feel, playing with your heart and soul, and also technique. Of course, you have to have good time. That's probably the hardest thing of all, steady tempo, and probably the great drummers are really born with it. I always keep the actual tempo in my head and then take it off from there, but always maintain the pulse. As long as you maintain that pulse, you can do anything. There are some good timekeepers who are boring as hell, and some who are very exciting and flashy, but have bad time. You have to get somewhere in between and add the fire that needs to be added, and also give the guys a solid bass for them to latch on to. If the drummer is not on, say at a live gig, it's very hard for the band to cook. It's a little better if he's rushing than dragging. As long as it's not too outrageous, at least it gives everyone some energy. On records, it's a little more critical and you have to lay back a bit more and be exact. Being a drummer is a lot of responsibility because it's a very physical thing, and if you're tired or something, you really have to push yourself."

Soloing is not one of Seraphine's favorite things. "I think drum solos are basically kind of boring," he explains. "People seem to love them at live concerts, but the average person wants to hear a drummer play as loud and fast as he can. I'm not putting people down for it, because obviously they don't have the same knowledge as somebody who has made his life out of drums. If you're that kind of drummer, that's alright. But if you're a really creative drummer, and try to really say something, it's difficult.

When I do a solo, I try to really say something, and at the end of it, I'll give them their razzle dazzle bullshit and get them up on their feet. That's not to say I haven't done some solos I'm really proud of, but solos can end up being an exercise in ego. A solo is hard in the sense of your playing the changes. Say your sax just took a 32 bar solo right through the changes. A real challenge for a drummer is to do the same and musically say something and come right back in on the 33rd bar. Normally, the way most drum solos are structured, they don't do that. What I try to do is lay something down that's related to the song, unless I'm doing a showboat solo, because people like that kind of solo." Ultimately, Seraphine prefers recording

to concerts. "Playing live is creative, but the actual creation of what brings people to that point, is the record," he states. "When I first started recording, it freaked me out because it's kind of an unnatural way to play. You really can't have the drums too live because you get all these weird overtones fighting each other and you lose isolation, but I've gotten so used to it now that I really enjoy it. I prefer the studio because it's more controlled and sensitive. I'm lucky because I play with a group that plays good music. I guess if you were a

session guy who played one enjoyable session out of ten, you wouldn't feel that way — you'd be really itching to get out on the road."

Seraphine, himself, would enjoy doing more sessions. "I guess people just assume that I don't have the time because I don't get that many calls. I would really like to do more," he says enthusiastically, having worked on Helen Reddy's latest release.

But Seraphine admits that his time is, in fact, scant, and one of the things often pushed in the background is

MODERN DRUMMER

DEC-JAN, 1979
$1.75

A Contemporary Publication Exclusively for Drummers

DANNY SERAPHINE:
The Rhythm of Chicago

MD Talks with
Jethro Tull's
BARRIEMORE
BARLOW

MICHAEL CARVIN

Jazz Purist
Spreading the Word

CHARLEY PERRY:
On Brushes

How To
Weatherproof
Your
Cases

Shop Hoppin'

Percussion-NY

BOB MOSES:
On Drum Set Concepts

practicing. "I don't really have any set practice times anymore. If we're getting ready to do an album, I'll start practicing maybe an hour every day, or two hours one day and then nothing for two or three days. I don't have a schedule anymore. When I do have the chance, I just go through the single strokes and then do the Buddy Rich exercises I've learned. One exercise Bob Tilles taught me, which I'm pretty sure is a Buddy Rich exercise, is hard to describe, but you do single strokes and then flip your wrists back as far as

back down, which is really hard, but good discipline. I really try to loosen up before doing a show so that when I go for something, I don't stiffen up and play with my arms instead of wrists. You don't need to practice really, if you're on the road a lot, because you're playing all the time. I would learn things, weird, complicated things, and try to pull them off on a gig. They would never come out, and then two years later, all of a sudden, they would come out without my thinking consciously. If there's a special thing I want to try for, a sound or

opportunity to do it enough. I really have to think back now, but if I do a few sessions, it starts coming back to me." Clinics are also something that Seraphine has not had time for, although, he admits, "I'm not really a clinic man, anyway. I don't feel that comfortable doing them, and my reading has gone downhill. Most of those cats can read better than I now, anyway." Seraphine has done clinics in the past and says that if he were to do them again, he would, "just try to get my approach across — the philosophy and what I think is important. Normally you find that 90% of the clinic is answering questions about recording and how you get this sound and that sound and what to look for. A clinic really amounts to the people attending and what they want to know."

Seraphine has endorsed Slingerland for seven years, for they have managed to fulfill all his needs. "I prefer Slingerland because they're really good drums," he declares. "They're strong and good for recording and live performances.

"Snares are really finicky. I've had some crazy days with snare drums, but I've been dampening it with tissue — Kleenex and tape in different amounts. I'll just line the inner rim with tissue and tape it. That's kind of a nice way to dampen it because it's still kind of a live thing you get.

"Basically, I like wood drums because they're warmer sounding. I hate plexiglass drums because I think they sound plastic and I think no matter what kind of music you're playing, a warmer sound is always going to be better.

"Right now, I'm using five toms: 8", 10", 12", 14" and sometimes, instead of a 16",

they can go, using conventional grip. Just one at a time for a few minutes. It's a pretty good loosening up exercise. Normally I'll do four strokes in one hand or triplets hand to hand or I'll go from one to ten on each hand. Another exercise I'll do is start with one, each hand, then I'll go to two, then three, four, five, six, seven, up to ten, and then

a special groove, I'll sit down and think it out in my head and just experiment. "When you're studying, you need to practice a lot. It would be good for me to study again now. I should take a refresher course in reading, but I don't have the time. If you can read, that really helps. I'm not a good reader anymore because I just haven't had the

I use a 14" X 14" for timpani rolls and things you can't really do on concert toms."

Seraphine alternates between a 20" and a 24" bass drum, since they suit his tuning purposes. "I tend to use smaller drums because you can tune them lower and they're still high enough worlds — the finesse and hard rock. I have to have a stick that's not too heavy nor too light. It's a kind of in between and fairly long stick, but it's not super heavy. I don't believe in super heavy sticks because I can't pull off what I want to do. By the same token, I can't use too light of a stick because I go the house and say, 'I've got something for you to try.' Different ways— the clear head with the black dot and all sorts of things. I had told him I wouldn't play anything plastic because they're just not warm sounding to me, so finally, after a lot of experimentation, he came up with the FiberSkyn. For the studio,

"Basically, I like wood drums because they're warmer sounding. I hate plexiglass drums because I think they sound plastic and I think no matter what kind of music you're playing, a warmer sound is always going to be better."

where they're not too tubby. I found that to be good in the studio, because when you get drums that are too big, in tuning them low, by the time you get to that low tom, it's dead."

Seraphine is looking forward to being even more articulate on Chicago's current recording, which, by the time of this article's printing, will have already been released. To him, that means perfection tuning, which he does solely by ear. "I'm going to take more time and really concentrate on each individual tom and get a pitch that's perfect in relation to the others. It's hard to do because you'll get a pitch relationship between the toms and they won't all actually sound good by themselves. So, you really have to find the right tonal scale, and since I only use ear, I start with the high tom and get it sounding good, but high enough so that the low one isn't so low it's nonexistent." Slingerland is making Seraphine a stick now which has his name on it. "I like it because I'm caught between two through them too fast."
Seraphine's relationship at Zildjian is also outstanding, and Lenny DiMuzio hand picks and sends him cymbals. "I tell him what I want and he's got really good ears and just sends me the stuff. For the last album, he sent me a 25-year-old crash cymbal, handmade, and that sounded great. It was a small 16" crash and it was crystal clear. I like to use pang cymbals for certain things like accents because they're really powerful, or a funky kind of a ride cymbal. I generally use two crashes, an 18" and a 16" and maybe a 20" ride and the pang. It really depends on what kind of sound I want, though."

An old established friendship with Remo provided Seraphine with the change from calf head to FiberSkyn because, as Seraphine relays, smiling, "Remo and I got to be real close and he said to me one day, 'I can't have you playing calf heads — I just can't have that.' Remo and I used to have a lot of fun," he recalls. "He would come over to they're really great and I use them live too, because I want to reproduce my sound."

In detailing what Seraphine thinks is his sound, he describes, "What I try to do is get a fairly melodic sound, which I think I've done. I have a trademark sound which is what I get with the concert tom-tom and the way I record them. I try to get a very melodic, rich, full sound, the entire spectrum of the frequency range. The high frequency range with the cymbals, really crisp and clean; the bass drum, very low, but also very punchy; the snare drum, mid range and cutting, but there; and then the toms, very melodic and full."

Another attempt at reproducing his album sound live is Seraphine's use of headphones on stage. "I had this problem in the early days when we went from clubs to nice concert halls to the toilets, which I consider the big arenas and forums because they sound like toilet bowls. I had this idea that maybe headphones would help

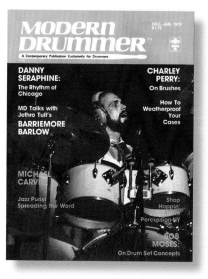

You have to be aggressive and sell yourself and realize that there are certain compromises you have to make down the line. When you're starting out, you have to get a perspective. Find a good teacher, study and learn music. Jam a lot while you're studying so you get the best of both worlds," Seraphine advises. "You get to learn the technical part of the drums and all of music and understand what is going on around you.

because it would be direct sound rather than hearing sound bouncing off walls, or not hearing at all. Now I'm used to playing the big arenas and outdoor places. The headphones really help a lot, because if you get the mix right, you can hear your foot, which is usually a problem unless you're recording. You don't have to play as hard. To me, you can only play drums so hard and then they get distorted. You can only hit the cymbal so hard and then it loses its resonance. The problem with playing live is that everyone is turning up so loud because they can't hear themselves and it becomes a big battle. The monitor philosophy really doesn't work because when you have monitors, they feed into the microphones and you get feedback and lose clarity." Equipped with his own mixing board for the headphones, Seraphine admits that it is tricky and could be a nightmare if done incorrectly. However, he feels it is the solution to a problem and more drummers should use the headphone system.

Seraphine is constantly experimenting and has already asked Slingerland to send him a double-headed drumset to try on the next album. "It's a little bit harder to get on

a double-headed set of drums because it's harder to control the ring," he says. "If you tune them too loosely, they ring too much and if you tune them too high, they sound tinny, but it can be done. It's just a little more work. Actually, double-headed drums are a little easier to play because they have rebound and they're faster, which is the aspect I like about them."

He has also just recently taken a set with double-bass drums out on tour. "The first time I ever played double-bass was one night when I was in a club and jammed with a couple of guys from Rufus. The kid whose set it was had double bass drums, so I figured I'd just give it a try. I never played them because I've always been against them. I didn't think they would play as sensitively and that it was an unbalanced way to play. People tend to overuse them, but I jammed with them. I do a lot of double-time things, and noticed with the double bass drums, I could get that locomotive groove happening and play rhythms off the top. I thought that was kind of interesting. In Chicago, there are a lot of power rock and roll grooves that we get into that double bass drums really fit into well. So I tried it this tour. Even for

solos it's good because the people really like when you get into that locomotive, double-time thing on the bass drum, as long as you don't over use it. If you use it in the right spots, it's great. If you use it in the wrong spots, it sounds like a guy falling down the stairs with a set of timpani. Guys like Louie Bellson and Ginger Baker are really great on it. It's really nice, even if I'm just playing four on the other bass drum, it still has more punch to it. I really had thought it would be uncomfortable to play, but it's not. In fact, I find it more comfortable and balanced. Sometimes I'll just use the other bass drum to augment what I'm playing, like to accent a crash. I still use the hi-hat when it's necessary and in the same places I used it before. It's just that now I have a new alternative and I enjoy that."

One of the first to use Syndrums, although never on a Chicago recording, Seraphine feels that they have been overused in the industry and therefore no longer accompany his live set-up. "I was using them as a solo instrument for a tune and it really killed the audience because I would get the sustain thing happening in a 6/8 rhythm and play off of it. I think for low tom sounds they can be really nice. You can get really low and mix it in with the actual low tom and it's kind of interesting. If used right, I think Syndrums are fine. But just give me a good set of drums that I can tune and are comfortable to play. That's enough for me. They can make all the toys they want, but really, drums are basically drums.

"I'm not the drum fanatic I used to be," Seraphine admits. "I used to eat, sleep and drink drums." Finding the need to expand his interests, Seraphine has become more and more involved with the production aspect of music. He and his partner, David "Hawk" Wolynsky of Rufus, with whom he writes lyrics, have formed a production company, hoping to contribute talent to the music industry in that way also. "The production company has to establish itself. We have to make a couple of hit records and then I want to produce just good music. We have to prove ourselves and I figure, once you prove yourself, you get more freedom to do what you want to do."

Obviously learning that lesson first hand, Seraphine is appreciative of the freedom his success has given him both musically and personally. Although it is evident that he can easily obtain any equipment, and admits that he really has more than he knows what to do with, Seraphine is neither pompous nor pretentious. "When I started to make money, I always felt that I had to give something back. So , I opened a live club in Chicago. It has things I didn't have when I was a kid, like nice dressing rooms and a good, big stage with a nice sound system. Young bands can play there. It hasn't totally turned out to be what I wanted it to be. With the music I would like to put into it, I would go broke, the Freddie Hubbards and big bands. Having tried that, now it's more of a rock club, but it's still a place where young bands can get a start. Cheap Trick and The Boys started out there. Billy Joel played there between the period of the Stranger album and 52nd Street."

Seraphine's sincere concern for musicians and the state of the art all stems back to his overall philosophy. "I think you really have to have the right philosophy when you get into music.

When I got into music, it wasn't to become a millionaire. My motivation was my love for music and I think you have to do it for that reason. There are so many musicians and rock bands who get together just to make it because that's the thinking in today's music. You have to be aggressive and sell yourself and realize that there are certain compromises you have to make down the line. When you're starting out, you have to get a perspective. Find a good teacher, study and learn music.

Jam a lot while you're studying so you get the best of both worlds," Seraphine advises. "You get to learn the technical part of the drums and all of music and understand what is going on around you.

That was an important part of my playing. I understood what I was playing and it made me get better. Once I knew what I was playing, I wanted to move onto the unknown. Study. Practice a lot. Drums are a very disciplined instrument because you're using both legs and both arms and have to get them going together. Play along with records, anything. If you really contribute something to music, that's really an accomplishment, and I think that's what you really have to push for."

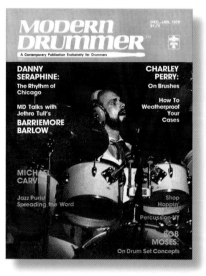

2011: Danny Seraphine: Update

By Bob Girouard

It seems that since Danny Seraphine made a comeback of sorts of the 2006 Modern Drummer Festival, he's kicked the current phase of his drumming career into high gear, appearing at events like Drummers for Jesus, the 2009 Chicago Drum Show, and a Terry Kath tribute, and making a memorable appearance at Donn Bennett's Drum Shop in Seattle. Seraphine's autobiography, Street Player: My Chicago Story, and new DVD, The Art of Jazz Rock Drumming, have also hit the shelves recently. MD sat down with the legendary drummer to find out more about his latest projects.

MD: How do you feel the reception to your recent comeback has been?

Danny: The Modern Drummer Festival is something I'll never forget. It was really gratifying; it's hard to explain all the emotions. I thank everyone at MD, along with my equipment sponsors, DW, Remo, Zildjian, and Pro-Mark. But most of all I thank the drummers of the world who welcomed me back. When I think about it, it still gives me chills. The reception out there has been incredible.

I used to be nervous doing clinics. I'd rather play in front of 50,000 people than fifty drummers, you know? I do a lot of clinics, and I feel the love. There are some guys who look at you and think, I'm faster than he is. But nearly all the drummers I've played to are those who've been influenced by my early stuff and are big followers of the jazz-rock genre. It's an incredible genre for drummers—really liberating.

MD: Since your departure from Chicago, you've done some very cool projects, including producing recording artists and Broadway shows. Were those rewarding experiences for you? And what made you want to get back in the game, so to speak?

Danny: I always try to do something that moves me artistically and spiritually. At that point in time I was kind of in exile from music. For the Broadway show, I was approached to find investors, which I had never done before. Because of my musical pedigree, I ended up getting involved with cast-soundtrack albums.

I was involved with two shows between 2003 and 2005. One was Bombay Dreams, which was written and composed by Andrew Lloyd Webber and A.R. Rahman [Slumdog Millionaire]. The second was called Brooklyn. Both were incredible, with great scores, but when you get a lukewarm review on Broadway, it's the kiss of death.

At the same time, I produced some really great but unknown artists. As far as success, some of it was there but not all the way there, if you know what I mean. The lightbulb finally went off in my head, saying, Get back to playing. Not to mention that many people were asking me why I wasn't drumming. So I took some private refresher lessons with Joe Porcaro to work on my technique, and here I am.

MD: Full Circle, by your group California Transit Authority, is a killer calling card. You've kept the spirit of the original Chicago sound—especially of the first two albums—with a fresh, adventurous approach. And your guitarist, Marc Bonilla, practically channels Terry Kath. How difficult was it to find players who could give you what you were looking for?

Danny: If you talk to most of the younger cats, it all started with jazz-rock being the catalyst to becoming musicians. Marc was a big fan of Terry's, and he's the best guitarist I've played with since then. Keyboard player Peter Fish is a brilliant arranger. Our other keyboardist, Ed Roth—what a player! Bassist Mick Mahan has a great pocket. And then you've got singer Larry Braggs, who brings the R&B thing to the Chicago thing. CTA is a labor of love.

MD: What's going on with the band at present?

Danny: We're working on a new record called Promises. It's all originals except for a Blood, Sweat & Tears song and a Chicago song that I cowrote. They're all in the jazz-rock genre, which nobody's doing. It's a dying art, you know?

MD: A very cool thing about your DVD is the way you present your approach to the beats and fills you created, within the framework of your music. You cut in and out of each song with a conversational, easy-to-understand

Consequently, it sounded like Chicago on steroids. It was, to say the least, powerful.

MD: Your own playing continues to amaze. Stylistically, you have so much of Buddy Rich in your execution, but you rock like crazy at the same time.

Danny: Yeah, there's Buddy and a lot of Gene Krupa. I think I was only ten or eleven when The Gene Krupa Story soundtrack came out. I really learned how to play by listening to it. Buddy told me personally that Gene influenced him. I'm really blessed, because they were the foundation of my playing—as well as rock guys like Hal Blaine, Mitch Mitchell, Ringo Starr, Dino Danelli…. All these guys had a style. My ambition was always to integrate elements from whoever I learned from.

MD: You have that perfect combination of being self-

> The *Modern Drummer* Festival is something I'll never forget. It was really gratifying; it's hard to explain all the emotions. I thank everyone at *MD*, along with my equipment sponsors, DW, Remo, Zildjian, and Pro-Mark. But most of all I thank the drummers of the world who welcomed me back.

analysis. How did you want to make your video different from the many you've come across?

Danny: Well, the lion's share of credit goes to [Drum Workshop and Drum Channel founder] Don Lombardi. Like the guy who cowrote my book, Adam Mitchell, Don really helped me craft the DVD. We discussed the approach, and he stayed on it diligently. We wanted to entertain as well as educate. For twenty-three years with Chicago, I wasn't allowed to talk, and now you can't shut me up! [laughs] It's been fun reaching out to the drummers of the world, and I want them to know that I'm approachable on anything.

MD: The disc also highlights four great cuts: "Introduction," "Antonio's Love Jungle," "I'm a Man," and "25 or 6 to 4." You stay faithful to the arrangements, but at the same time you aren't afraid to stretch with solos. It's almost like a jazz concept in a big band format. Was that your emphasis from the start?

Danny: That's a good analogy. Interestingly, on the new CD we have a full brass section. It kind of happened by accident. In the summer of 2006 I was asked to play at a benefit for the photographer Lissa Wales. At the time I couldn't pull a horn section together, so Marc Bonilla suggested he play some of the horn parts on guitar.

taught and studying formally. Do you feel that's a must for today's young players?

Danny: I don't like to preach, but there's nothing I can say to these "chops cats." I appreciate what they're doing, and they're giving me all kinds of ideas. But you know what? It's not just about the drummer world; it's about the rest of the world. Even with today's styles, the drummer's role is to hold it together. I don't care if it's country, alt rock, metal, whatever—it's about the groove. That is absolutely first and foremost, and once you get that in your head, everything else is easy. Furthermore, the other musicians in the band will appreciate you.

MD: Many of us are still puzzled by your dismissal from Chicago in 1990.

Danny: The dismissal thing was bullshit. I got caught on the wrong end of a power play. What happened was during the drug-and-alcohol days, I stepped on a lot of people's toes. Eventually, everybody got straight again— which I was very proud of achieving for myself—and all of a sudden they wanted to put me in the background. In other words, it was like, "Go back on the drums and shut up!" First, it was patronizing. And second, that's just not my way. The agenda was "disguised" by my playing, and I believed it at first. But I realized that, yes, there might have been some truth [to the accusation] that I was too involved with the business at the time. But these guys were like brothers. Sure, there were typical band dynamics, but that's the case in every band. All in all, the whole experience made me a better drummer and a better person. I'm not wealthy like I used to be, but I'm rich in other ways, so I'm grateful.

MD: When you first arrived on the scene, it is well known that Buddy Rich mentioned you, along with Bobby Colomby, as among his favorite drummers. He made no secret about his disdain for rock drummers, so this was a real badge of honor. Has it remained something that you consciously or subconsciously uphold to this day?

Danny: Without a doubt! It's like getting an endorsement from God. Buddy was a good friend, and it was such a great honor to be acknowledged by your drum hero, not to mention in front of millions of people who heard him say that on television.

MD: You're presenting a fresh take on a style that's been ignored for a while. You have something special with CTA, but given the state of today's technology over the years, it seems you're comfortable with any drum configuration—from early five-piece setups with two floor toms to two mounted rack toms to the three-rack, three-floor, two-kick setup you're currently using. How have you been able to master all of them?

Danny: I think that's kind of the fun of it—adjusting to what you have in front of you and making it work for you. I try to use what I have within the framework of the music—for instance, with Chicago, using a lot of colors and cymbals, and now using different-size drums with CTA. Although I love playing with a small bass drum, I'm now using a 23″ bass drum, and it's deep.

MD: Did you spend a lot of time mastering the double pedal before integrating it into your kit?

Danny: Yes. I worked with Chuck Flores on independence and foot technique, and we worked on developing my left foot. I mean, today guys like Thomas Lang play things with their feet that most drummers can't do with their hands. I love practicing and using a double pedal. It's a constant challenge, but I feel I'm doing so much more in the process and

> Practicing, for me, depends a lot on where I am at the moment. I do most of it on pads. There's a discipline on pads that you don't have on drums. Then I go over to the drums and experiment. Yes, I believe practice is essential—if you want to keep moving forward and learning, you need to practice and listen.

and the constant media barrage, it's hard to get any art form, especially music, to stick. Do you think you can crack the mass market?

Danny: I don't know. It's so frightening. But I think what we can do is rally the troops, so to speak—people who really miss and want good music. And if they like it, perhaps they'll buy a CD and tell their friends, who'll tell their friends. It will be difficult, but I'm up to the task. I have to be pragmatic about my expectations, and my priority is getting the band out there and touring. I love what I do and want to keep doing it. I also want to help others in the process and share whatever I know with other drummers. I've had the chance to do things that most people can only dream of.

MD: In looking at the many photos and videos of you

integrating it into my style at the same time.

MD: The positioning of your drums and cymbals is set by your arm length and reach—much like Buddy Rich. Do you subscribe to the "no wasted motion" theory?

Danny: Oh, yeah. That was the beauty of Buddy. He had hardly any wasted motion, until he went into super-overdrive. His overdrive was, of course, beyond human; he had a gear that no one except maybe Billy Cobham had, where everybody watching would think, How did he do that? But even though you might not be able to duplicate what they'd be doing, you could still get something out of it. My advice: Watch and learn.

MD: It's obvious that you've been well schooled in

drum rudiments. But a lot of your style is about feel. Do you think about rudiments or about sound when you apply a sticking pattern to the music?

Danny: I don't think in terms of rudiments. I think only in terms of sound and feel. Even though I'm not thinking in terms of RLRR, LRLL, however, subconsciously I am using rudiments to facilitate what I need to do.

MD: What's your stand on formal practicing on the drumset?

Danny: Practicing, for me, depends a lot on where I am at the moment. I do most of it on pads. There's a discipline on pads that you don't have on drums. Then I go over to the drums and experiment. Yes, I believe practice is essential—if you want to keep moving forward and learning, you need to practice and listen.

For more on Danny Seraphine, go to moderndrummer.com

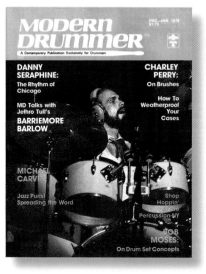

2019: Ready For the Next Phase

By Jeff Potter

Danny Seraphine fueled a long list of classic tracks in his twenty-three years as a member of Chicago, inspiring generations of drummers in the process. Since returning in 2006 from a long performing hiatus, he has been grooving in peak form with his current band, CTA, as heard on its latest CD, Sacred Ground. Also recently hitting the shelves are Seraphine's autobiography, Street Player: My Chicago Story, and instructional DVD, The Art of Jazz Rock Drumming. Danny is honored in Modern Drummer magazine's Influences feature this month; here he expands upon some of the topics covered in that piece.

MD: You've influenced so many drummers, but who influenced you?

Danny: I learned from Gene Krupa, playing along with The Gene Krupa Story. I also played along with records like Cozy Cole's "Topsy Part 2." Then I really got into Buddy Rich and, later, Elvin Jones and Max Roach. For rock, I was influenced by Hal Blaine, and later Mitch Mitchell was a guy I really listened to a lot and could identify with—the way he would stretch out with Jimi Hendrix. And Dino Dinelli—I loved his playing and style on those early Rascals records. He had that real swagger.

I loved all of James Brown's records, especially Live at the Apollo with Clayton Fillyau. Local Chicago funk drummers also influenced me, including a drummer named Dwight Kalb. He had such a great feel. I absorbed that, and I still hear that in my own playing. The "Make Me Smile" groove was a derivative of Dwight's playing. It's a groove I picked up in Chicago, and it's still with me. It's a part of me—I think it's one of the better parts of my playing. It gives me the pocket that maybe a lot of chops players don't have.

MD: After your long absence from drumming, you rediscovered what it really meant to you.

Danny: First and foremost, it's what God put me on earth to do; it's my calling. To run away from your calling and what you do best for so long…it can be destructive. I always just had an empty feeling. When I play, I feel complete. And when I've finished playing I feel complete too. To not have that for so long, I was starved. I want to get out with CTA and spread the music even more, because it's really a great band. This band is a true force. Sacred Ground includes some of the best things I've ever played on. Unlike the first CD, most of it is original material. It represents the evolution of where we started with CTA—trying to reinvigorate and keep the jazz-rock genre alive, because it's been badly neglected.

MD: CTA's debut CD, Full Circle, included reworkings of Chicago classics.

Danny: Some of my CTA bandmates wanted to get away from it, but I embrace it. When I first left Chicago—when I was fired—I didn't want anything to do with it. I just wanted to be left alone and do something else; I didn't want to play. I was very bitter and disillusioned with the music business. It's a very unfriendly, corrupted industry. They're carnivores: They eat their own.

But I'm very grateful for the great career I've had up to this point, and I have a lot more music left in me.

MD: What were the greatest challenges in returning from the hiatus?

Danny: The physical endurance part was one challenging factor. My confidence was another. That took a while. The Modern Drummer Festival performance of 2006 was a really big thing for me. It was like the drummers of the world welcoming me back, embracing what I've done. It made me realize that people hadn't forgotten me and that I had a lot more to contribute. It was a great, great night for me that I'll never forget.

The drums are the most physically challenging instrument by far, especially if you play double bass drums. And I love that part of it—keeping in shape, staying healthy. At sixty-five, that can be very challenging. Things do wear out. [laughs] I'm dealing with some ailments;

age takes its toll. Nonetheless, I'm going to play until I can't play anymore. Every drummer that I know close to my age is having physical problems. For example, if you're playing matched as opposed to traditional grip, you're going to have troubles in your forearms rather than under your thumb, where you hold the fulcrum in traditional grip.

MD: Has alternating techniques helped minimize the repetitive stress?

Danny: Yes, definitely. I've always switched grips, even several times within a song. I love traditional grip. I love the fact that my left hand sounds different from my right. Some people strive for the hands to sound exactly the same with matched grip, but I like the different colorations that you can do with your left hand. It's important to have traditional grip in your arsenal. It's a whole other range of colors in your palette.

MD: What's next?

Danny: I feel like I'm about to go into another phase. That's the great thing about drumming and all music: It's ever-changing, and there's always something to learn from someone else. It's beautiful that, as drummers, we openly share licks and grooves. Each of us has our own DNA, our own stamp on the music. Someone could try to play "Make Me Smile" the same way, but it's just not going to be the same, and vice versa for me trying to play a Buddy Rich or Mitch Mitchell thing.

It's a great thing about what we do, the realization that our licks and grooves are just passing through us. Yeah, we might be known for them, but I got my influences from other people, and I've influenced a lot of drummers in turn. It's a gratifying thing when someone says to me, "I started playing because of you." It makes it worthwhile and gives me fuel to keep going, keep getting better, keep my playing young.

LEGENDARY DRUMMER INDUCTED ROCK AND ROLL

Pioneering jazz-rock drummer/composer/author and founding member of the Grammy award-winning rock group, Chicago, Danny Seraphine was officially inducted into the Rock and Roll Hall of Fame on Friday, April 8, 2016 at Brooklyn's Barclays Center.

Worldwide, Chicago has sold in excess of 122 million albums and has earned an estimated twenty-two gold, eighteen platinum, and eight multi-platinum albums. A long-time endorser of DW Drums, pedals, and hardware, Seraphine played a California Custom Shop Collector's series drumset in a new, retro-inspired White Crystal finish at the induction ceremony. Seraphine designed the kit with DW executive vice president and drum designer, John Good, to emulate the sets he played in the '70s. The kit, which includes a vintage-style "rail" tom mount and single-headed toms, "Looks and feels like the original, only better," commented Seraphine.

"This is a career milestone for Danny and we wanted to make him something really special to commemorate the occasion. He's been such an important part of

DANNY SERAPHINE INTO THE HALL OF FAME 2016

DW's history as a company, and we're immensely proud to have been a small part of Chicago's amazing journey," remarked Good.

"Danny is truly a music industry legend," said Drum Workshop Inc. founder, Don Lombardi. "I can't say enough about his impact on the drumming community and the entire DW family congratulates him on his induction into the Rock and Roll Hall of Fame."

The Rock and Roll Hall of Fame induction ceremony and performances aired on HBO on April 30, 2016.

Influences

Danny Seraphine: Integral

By Jeff Potter

At a time when jazz and rock drumming camps were largely polar, Danny Seraphine integrated his skills in both genres into a fresh, vibrant sound that launched megahits. Gregg Bissonette called him "one of my drumming heroes," and Steve Smith told MD, "Chicago was one of my favorite bands when I was in high school; I bought all of the early records and used to practice to them all the time."

When the brass-rock unit Chicago burst out with its 1970 sophomore release, Chicago II, the multiple hit singles rotated on the radio as frequently as weather updates. The now classic-rock staples, including the infectious "Make Me Smile," the rock-riffing "25 or 6 to 4," and the slow-dance prom favorite "Colour My World," filled the airwaves. Subsequently, several singles from the group's 1969 debut album, Chicago Transit Authority, were released, and the hits gushed forth again. In the following decades, that unstoppable multiplatinum momentum eventually made Chicago one of the highest-selling rock/pop acts of all time.

Drummer and cofounder Danny Seraphine was key in creating the sound and success of the long-lived ensemble, and he remains one of rock's most distinct drum voices. "In addition to blending styles," Seraphine says, "I wanted to be more than a timekeeper. I wanted to play musically within the song—to be a musical contributor, an integral part of the song." Chicago's sound was branded "jazz rock" partly due to its prominent brass section. More important, Seraphine's conceptual approach helped give the band its organic heart and soul. Although his grooves were structured from rock and R&B, Seraphine employed the swinging pulse, ensemble interplay, nimble chops, dynamics, fills, and breathing flow of a drummer steeped in jazz.

At age nine, Danny began playing drums in his native Chicago, gathering his earliest inspirations from jazzmen such as Cozy Cole and Gene Krupa. A self-proclaimed "street kid," the scrappy drummer quit high school and freelanced around town, plying his rock/R&B grooves. His first professional break came at fifteen years old, when he joined Jimmy Ford and the Executives, a local band that backed artists on Dick Clark's "Caravan of the Stars" road shows. At his first huge trial-by-fire road stop in Pittsburgh, the nervous teen drummer backed Chuck Berry and Lou Christie, among others. He was eventually let go, along with guitarist Terry Kath and reedman Walter Parazaider—an event that turned out to be great fortune. The dismissed musicians promptly recruited their own band, and by 1967 that core evolved into Chicago.

Parazaider introduced Seraphine to DePaul University percussion instructor Bob Tilles. Highly impressed with the budding drummer's talents, Tilles took Danny under his wing. Seraphine credits his mentor with helping him incorporate jazz into his rock concepts. "He saw something in me that I didn't see myself," he remembers. "He's the person I'm most grateful to." That concept bloomed further through Seraphine's later studies with Chuck Flores.

Casual fans may think of Chicago as a "singles" band, but the group's original signature format was double-LP releases featuring lengthy extended suites. Seraphine showed brilliance for orchestrating the dramatic arc of the lengthy pieces and also transferred that mastery to three-minute singles. Seraphine demonstrated a wide variety of drumming strengths that defined classic Chicago tracks. His gritty in-the-moment vitality jumps off the vinyl on cuts such as the driving seven-and-a-half-minute workout "I'm a Man," which also features his pumping solo. On "Free," he proves himself thoroughly at home with funky R&B. "South California Purples" showcases his funk/rock acumen, including a snapping syncopated bass foot. And his ease with odd time signatures is heard in the daunting 19/8 sections of "Introduction." "Saturday in the Park" is a prime example of Seraphine's artistry in creating imaginative orchestrated parts. On the monster hit "Does Anybody Really Know What Time It Is?" Danny straddles an irresistible shuffle/straight hybrid feel, while "Make Me Smile" opens with a soul syncopation setup, then drives ahead with an irresistible to-the-edge pulse. And on the later pop hit "Feelin' Stronger Every Day," he lays down a clean, grooving mid-tempo pocket. Digging beyond the hits, fans will also enjoy the drummer deftly steering complex arrangements on progressive cuts such as "Now That You've Gone," and

"A Hit by Varèse." An especially impressive drumming showcase is the album Chicago VII, which includes "Devil's Sweet," a number Seraphine cowrote. The ten-minute-plus opus captures the rare sound of the jazzy, colorful brush soloing that Danny honed via studies with the great Jo Jones. The track eventually morphs into fusion territory and climaxes with a probing solo employing sticks.

Also a master of fiery, effective fills, Seraphine has created multiple-bar setups that are often signature features in Chicago's arrangements. The drummer's tension-and-release licks snap the band into a higher gear much in the manner of a kicking big band drummer. An especially famed example is the four-bar mini-solo fill from "Make Me Smile." The unexpected broken-up syncopations suspend tension until finally releasing in quick, cathartic power triplets. It's an electrifying moment. A twenty-three-year-long ride with Chicago stretched until 1990, when Seraphine parted ways with the band due to a strained web of musical, personal, and business tensions. His tenure had earned eighteen gold and thirteen platinum albums, including fifty Top 40 hits. Disillusioned and burned out by the music industry, the exhausted drummer took a fifteen-year hiatus from performing. But in 2006, Seraphine became revitalized and doggedly resharpened his skills. He formed CTA, or California Transit Authority, a stellar lineup performing originals as well as reworkings of Chicago gems. Back in top form, he made a legendary appearance at the 2006 Modern Drummer Festival that was met with an overwhelming response. Soon after, CTA issued its aptly titled debut, Full Circle (2007), followed by Sacred Ground (2013).

Seraphine's contributions continue to inspire drummers of all ages. As an architect of the enduring, world-renowned Chicago sound, Danny has a legacy that holds a lofty place in the pantheon of rock drumming.

13

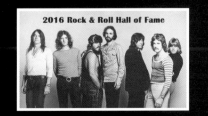

2016 Rock & Roll Hall of Fame

THE SONGS

Transcriptions

By Terry Branam

Danny's thoughts on...

By Mark Griffith

The groundbreaking drumming of Danny Seraphine will go down as one of the most important contributions to the catalog of contemporary 20th century music. He is a trailblazer of the jazz/rock genre, and is the archetype of that drumming style in every sense of the word. As a founding member of the legendary band Chicago, he has cast a wide influence on musicians of many ages. Danny's heart and soul is embedded within the essence of his instantly identifiable sound, and his playing is deeply woven into the fabric of Chicago's music.

Danny's playing style is a medley of big band and swing influences such as Jo Jones, Buddy Rich and Gene Krupa with a healthy dose of a funky rock and roll pocket. A classic crisp snare tone balanced with bright, articulate cymbals alongside a deep, thuddy bass drum compose Seraphine's groove element. High-pitched small toms counterbalance deep floor toms, bringing a strong melodic sensibility to his fill vocabulary. His big band-inspired approach is the perfect compliment to Chicago's horn-driven rock style, and his drumming within that group has made an unmistakable impact on modern drum set playing as we know it.

MUSIC KEY

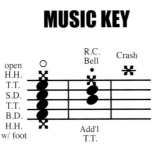

"Introduction" - *Chicago Transit Authority*

Ex 1 - "Introduction" is a great example of Chicago's powerful musical prowess as a group. Danny expertly leads the band through many tempo and meter changes, all while playing with great spirit and panache. He sets up the intro with a driving groove that leads with the snare drum. (0:00)

Ex 2 - The song shifts into a complex 19/8 meter, and Danny handles it with a perfectly composed part that plays off of the horn parts and the rhythm section figures at the same time. (1:14)

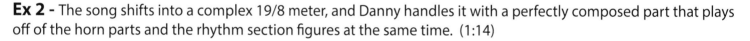

"Introduction" (continued)

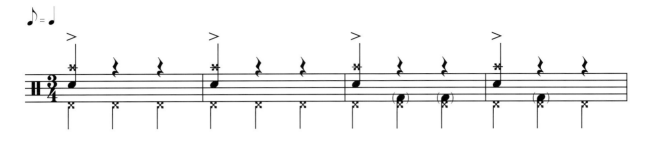

Ex 3 - After establishing another meter change to 3/4, Seraphine sets up a brisk jazz waltz feel to bring in the upcoming horn melody. (1:40)

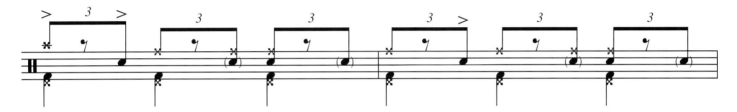

Ex 4 - Danny plays solo fills over the rhythm section figures after the big horn section near the end of the song. He plays some signature snappy accents on the snare and toms, and comes through with a big sixteenth note run down the drums to bring the band back in. (5:43)

Danny's Thoughts on "INTRODUCTION"

This was a powerful musical statement written by Terry Kath that set the tone for our band's first album. The song was inspired by the Don Ellis Big Band recording called "Autumn" which we were all listening to at the time.

"Introduction" embodied the essence of what Chicago was all about, and it demanded every bit of talent, musicianship, and concentration from everyone in the band. It consisted of three time changes 4/4, 19/8, and 3/4 as well as four tempo changes. The 19/8 section was counted like this 1-2-3, 1-2-3, 1-2, 1-2, 1-2, 1, 1-2, 1-2, 1-2 which adds up to 19/8.

I remember playing a gig at the Whiskey in 1968 and Jim Keltner was playing with Delaney and Bonnie & Friends that same night. They had just finished their soundcheck and they were hanging out to hear our sound check. We had just learned the "Introduction," and I still had those numbers written on my snare drum head on how to subdivide the 19/8 section. After our soundcheck Jim asked me how to count that odd time section, so I showed him my snare drum head. That was the beginning of a long friendship with Jim. He is a drummer I really admire.

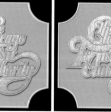

"Beginnings" - *Chicago Transit Authority*

Ex 5 - On the laid-back intro of "Beginnings", Danny plays a groovy fill and locks in with Cetera's melodic bass line to establish the pocket. Seraphine plays fills that anticipate the horn accents. (0:07)

"Beginnings" (continued)

Ex. 6 - This roundhouse fill picks up the energy in the first chorus. (1:09)

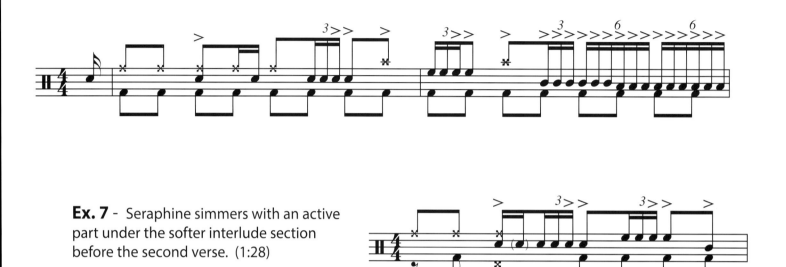

Ex. 7 - Seraphine simmers with an active part under the softer interlude section before the second verse. (1:28)

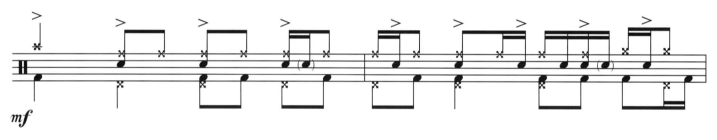

"Beginnings" (continued)

Ex. 8 - After the second interlude, Danny steps out front and plays a big four measure fill that sets the tone for the second half of the song. (3:02)

Danny's Thoughts on "BEGINNINGS"

When we were recording this, we were playing it all together live in the studio. I remember Terry Kath was in the walkway (air lock) between the control room and the big room playing acoustic guitar because there wasn't enough isolation booths for everyone in the band. Al Kooper filmed us recording this, but he later recorded over it, what a shame.

Many people feel this is one of my best drum parts and it is one of my favorites as well. I remember our producer James William Guercio in the booth exhorting me to play more and more fills because my toms were recorded and panned across the stereo image. That meant when I filled around the toms you could literally hear the drums go across the stereo spectrum. That was almost unheard of in those days, and subsequently became a standard in the industry. Our engineer Fred Catero and producer James William Guercio deserve all the credit for the groundbreaking drum recording techniques used on the CTA album.

I definitely did what he wanted and played as many fills as I could while trying to complement everything that was happening around me. We recorded pretty much everything live back then, because of that there was some horn leakage into the drum tracks. Then we would go back in and double and triple track the horn parts to fatten them up.

"Does Anybody Really Know What Time It Is?" - *Chicago Transit Authority*

Ex 9 - Danny fills around the unison horn accents on the intro of "Does Anybody Really Know What Time It Is?". He deftly navigates through the swing 5/8 meter before setting up a relaxed shuffle groove for the verse. (1:15)

"Does Anybody Really Know What Time It Is?" *(continued)*

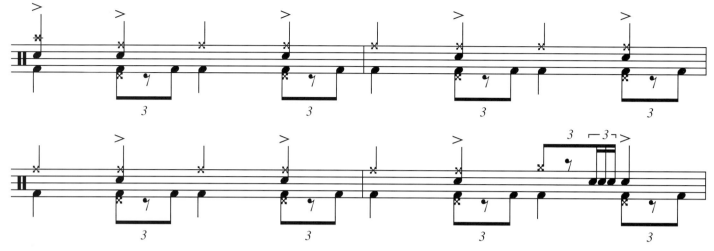

Ex 10 - Seraphine shows his big band chops in the verse by kicking the horn upbeats at the end of the measure with some slick fills. He adds momentum to the chorus by playing swing eighth notes on the bass drum. (2:01)

Verse

Chorus

Danny's Thoughts on "DOES ANYBODY KNOW WHAT TIME IT IS"

This was the first track we recorded as a band and I remember being scared and nervous. After hearing the playback in the control booth for the first time, I thought that I sounded terrible. Everyone has had that experience!

When I heard the song mixed several weeks later, I thought it sounded great. This is a great example of my fusion of big band and rock drumming.

The intro breaks into 5/4 time before a slight ritard back into 4/4. This drum part is a combination of the relaxed feel of Ringo in the verses and Buddy Rich & Gene Krupa in the choruses.

"Questions 67 & 68" - *Chicago Transit Authority*

Ex 11 - "Questions 67 & 68" opens with a melodic solo fill that bounces around the snare drum and toms. This song is a great example of the rapport that Seraphine and Cetera had on drums and bass. They lay down a sturdy foundation under the majestic horns and Terry Kath's shredding guitar. The band plays a ritard at the end of the section before the verse hits, adding a dramatic effect. (0:00)

"Questions 67 & 68"(continued)

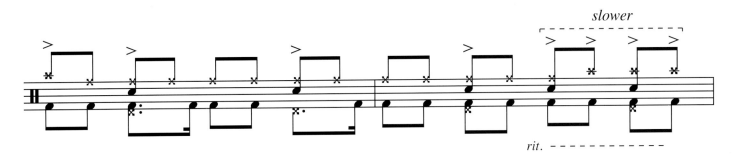

Ex 12 - He keeps the energy level high from the chorus to the interlude before the second verse by playing quick fills around the drums. (1:27)

Ex 13 - The drums and bass push the instrumental bridge with a dotted eighth and sixteenth rhythm. Danny plays a fill that shifts the band into gear for a double-time feel. (2:31)

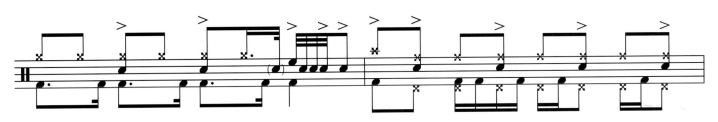

"Questions 67 & 68" (continued)

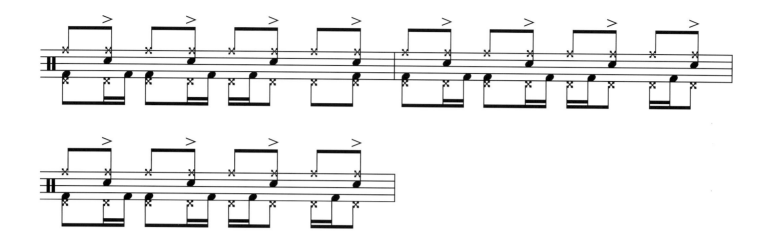

Ex 14 - Danny plays a blazing thirty-second note fill before the ritard into the last verse. (3:24)

Danny's Thoughts on "QUESTIONS 67 & 68"

This became a signature Chicago track. The drum part opens with a two beat triplet fill between my toms and snare which was a simple but very effective way to set up the song.

I love the classically influenced ritard into the first verse. Years later, David Foster and I used that same type of ritard on "Hard to Say I'm Sorry" from Chicago VXI.

I think that we gave "Questions 67 & 68" a much-needed lift by playing the double time section that combines a rock and jazz approach. I took many musical liberties when I was kicking the horn parts in this song like a big band drummer would. When I was kicking those horn parts in this song, that was one of the first times that I used that specific jazz approach combined with a rock feel.

"I'm A Man" - *Chicago Transit Authority*

Ex 15 - "I'm a Man" is a high-energy arrangement of a classic Spencer Davis track that is a great showcase for Seraphine's playing style. He locks in with Terry Kath's funky rhythm guitar part in the intro with a tight groove that has a short fill embedded into it. The other members of the band add percussion instruments one at a time creating a dense rhythmic ensemble. (0:10)

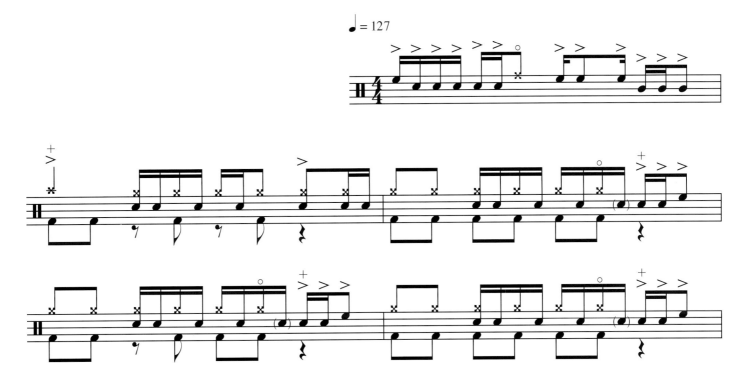

Ex 16 - The beat in the verse has a creative hi-hat accent on the "e" of beat four. (1:19)

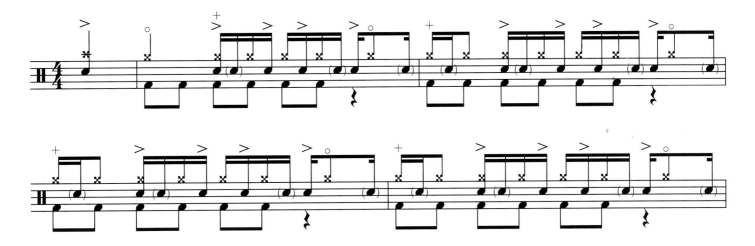

"I'm A Man"- (continued)

Ex 17 - On the chorus, the drums play a straight eighth note rhythm under the vocals for the first measure, then play a transitioning fill into the instrumental riff. The left hand adds extra notes on the third and fourth measures of the phrase to mix things up. (2:04)

Ex 18 - Later in the song, Danny gets an extended drum solo feature. He plays syncopated phrases that slowly build to a peak over the percussion and wah-wah guitar vamp. Seraphine's signature elements are all at work from over-the-barline phrasing, to the crisp six stroke rolls, complete with his right foot tapping eighth notes to hold everything together. It is an impressive display of Seraphine's legendary jazz/rock solo chops. (3:07)

"I'm A Man"- *(continued)*

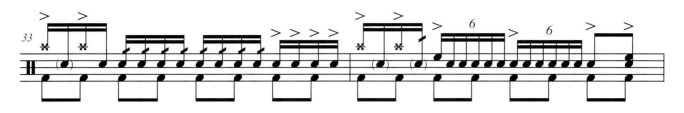

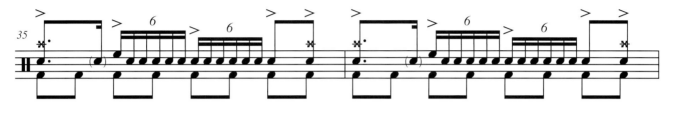

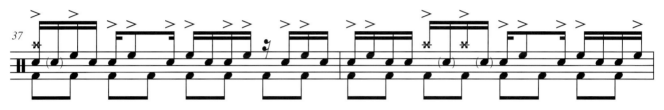

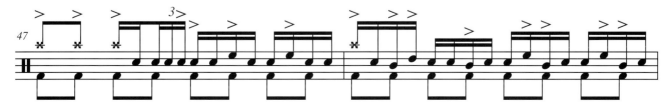

"I'm A Man"- (continued)

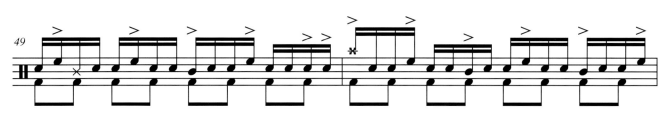

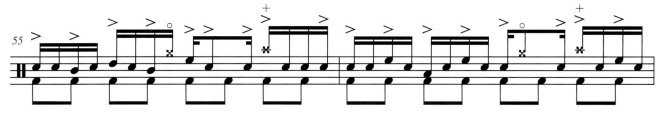

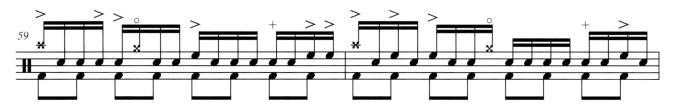

"One..."

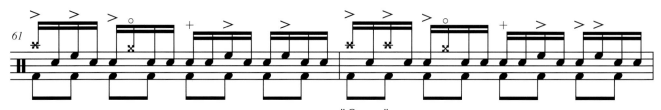

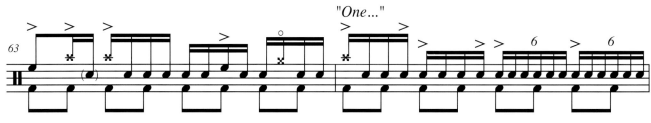

"Two..."

"Three..."

"Four..."

Danny's Thoughts on "I'M A MAN"

We used to play this tune in clubs when we were a cover band. When we decided to do a double album as our first release, which was unheard of at that time, we needed a little more material. The horn players were already playing percussion in the song, so we filled the tune out even a little more by adding the drum solo. It was a great thing for our producer to suggest, because I could play off of the percussion parts. Before the recording we had never performed this song with a drum/percussion solo. Therefore, what you are hearing on this record is the very first time that I had performed "I'm a Man" with a drum solo. Since then, it has not been performed without one. That solo definitely made this a signature tune for me.

This tune also has some influences of a great drummer named Joe Dukes. Joe used to play with Jack McDuff and I listened to him a lot. I haven't thought about Joe in a long time, I have to go back and revisit some Joe Dukes recordings, maybe you could suggest some to me?

MD: If you like Joe, you gotta hear him with Lonnie Smith too, there is a live one called "At The Club Mozambique," and a studio record called "Drive." The Jack McDuff "Live" is really good, and of course his own record called "The Soulful Drums of Joe Dukes."

"Movin' In" - *Chicago II*

Ex 19 - "Movin' In" is another prime example of Danny's relaxed, yet driving swing feel. He supports the vocals in the verse by not getting in the way with the groove, and answering with fills in the gaps. (0:20)

Ex 20 - When the band transitions to a double-time swing feel in the bridge, he lays down a mean Chicago-style shuffle. (1:15)

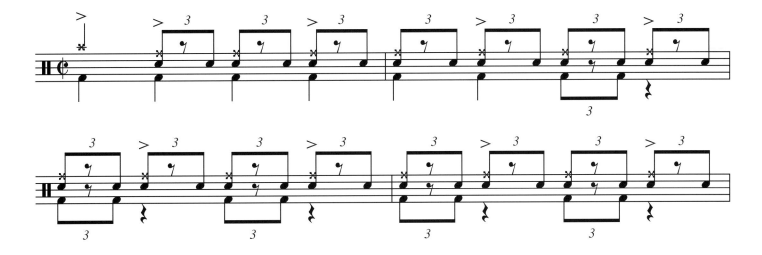

"Movin' In"(continued)

Ex 21 - Danny plays an uptempo jazz waltz on the outro tag that shows off his fast left hand technique. (3:49)

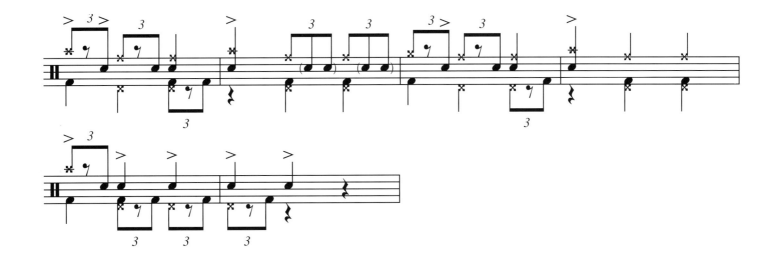

Danny's Thoughts on "MOVIN' IN"

This song and drum part really epitomizes my jazz/rock style of drumming. The half-time intro and verses parts are really loose and subtly suggests the swing section that comes later in the song. That way when we get to the horn solos (in the double time section,) the transition into it that Count Basie styled swing horn solo section is smooth. The 3/4 swing outro really brings it all home to the big band tradition. This was definitely a ground-breaking tune for a rock band to write and perform. Those transitions between jazz and rock or swing and straight eighth became (sort of) my specialty, that's what I do best.

MD: Making transitions is a problem that most drummers have. Whether it's getting from the verse to the chorus or the bridge, or just transitioning between a groove and a fill and back to the groove, that gives many drummers and bands a hard time. What kind of advice can you give regarding that?

Danny: You have to really lock into the pulse. In rock the pulse is really the quarter note, and in jazz the pulse is the swung eighth (triplet) feel. But when you make the transition between the two, you have to maintain that quarter note pulse without pounding it home. That's what can really screw up a jazz feel, and that's what lots of rock guys do, they pound the quarter note pulse, and that just destroys the swing.

Remember I grew up playing along to the soundtrack from the "Gene Krupa Story." So that laid the foundation for my sense of swing. I learned to swing at an inordinately young age. Then I started playing rock.

But when I am making transitions between two sections of a tune, I always try to keep the rhythmic relationship in mind. I would keep in mind what rhythmic context I am coming from, and what I am going to. I always try to match my fill to the rhythmic context that I am going into, but the fill also has to work with the musical section that I am playing presently, or coming out of.

A fill that suggests what is coming is like a passing tone in a chord, it's like a common denominator I guess. When I played "Wake Up Sunshine" I play a straight sixteenth fill that gets me into the rock section from the swing section. I will often use a fill to introduce the next musical section. I think one of my strong suits has always been my ability to make seamless transitions between different sections of music. Buddy did that a lot too, especially on stuff like "The West Side Story Suite."

"25 or 6 to 4" - *Chicago II*

Ex 22 - The iconic rock anthem "25 or 6 to 4" features an intriguing double-tracked drum part. One take has the drums playing straight time, with quarter notes on the hi-hat, 2 and 4 on the snare, and running eighth notes on the bass drum. Another overdubbed take has the drums playing fills and additions to the grooves. Danny comes in at the top of the song with only hi-hat and snare, then brings in constant eighths on the bass drum when the horns enter. (0:07)

Ex 23 - In the verse, the second drum set creates a unique rhythm by playing a five-stroke roll between the tom and snare drum that ends on an open hi-hat note. (0:26)

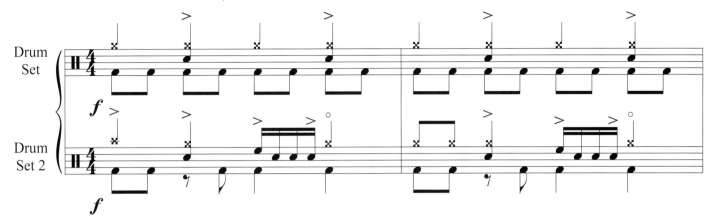

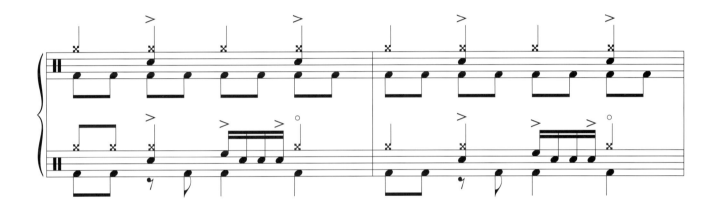

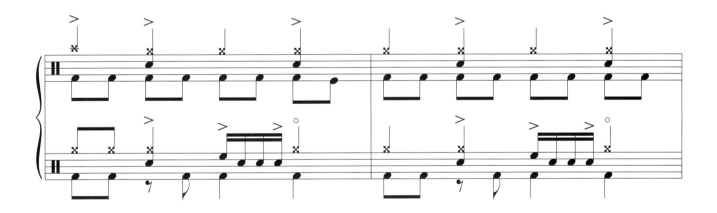

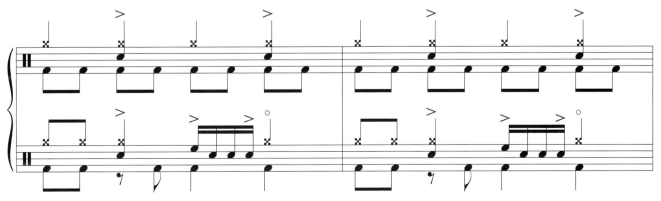

"25 or 6 to 4"(continued)

Ex 24 - The drums and bass switch to a half-time feel on the chorus. The double drum sets have a powerful effect with two ride cymbals, snare drums and bass drums playing off of each other in the stereo spectrum. (0:49)

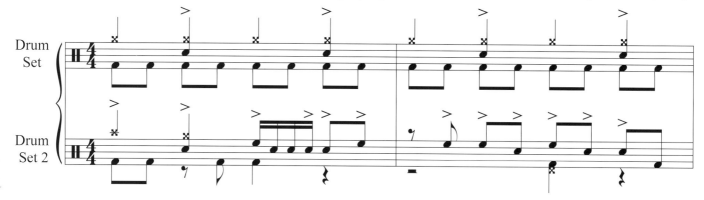

Chorus

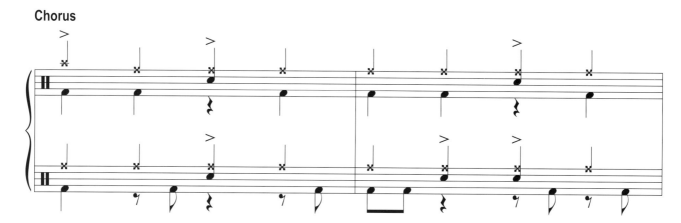

Danny's Thoughts on "25 OR 6 TO 4"

This is Chicago's best known track. I love the message of the lyrics. The way that Robert Lamm wrote that song, it really became (like) our "mission statement." The drum part was recorded as two different parts that you hear simutaneously. I had the idea of playing two separate drum parts, and James loved the idea. I played the first part with almost no fills. And then I played the second part with time and fills. You can hear me answering myself with fills and crashes between the separate parts.

During the solo you can hear me doubling the bell of the ride cymbal, and doubling the time in some sections which made the time feel really powerful. There are some little time rubs in the final version, if you listen really closely you can hear them, but the two drum parts sound really cool together. You almost have to listen to it on headphones to really hear it. You can hear the little five stroke rolls are on a different set and sound. Amazingly, the band was getting really pissed while we were

spending all of this time on two drum parts for the same song, so we just stopped. If we had completed what James and I were doing, we probably would have smoothed out some of the rough spots. But we stopped because the guys in the band thought we were crazy. Then when we were mixing the record, James put up both parts for us to hear at the same time, and they sounded incredible together, so James used them both.

"Saturday in the Park"- *Chicago II*

Ex 25 - The kick and snare play a funky rhythm in the intro that pairs nicely with Robert Lamm's piano part. (0:08)

Ex 26 - A brilliantly thought-out drum composition in the chorus highlights all of the different moving parts that make up the section. He goes back and forth between snare and tom figures that play off of the vocal melody and light hi-hat rhythms that add contrast and highlight the instrumental parts. At the end of the second chorus, he sets the band up with a heavy triplet fill to shift into swing time on the bridge. (1:36)

"Saturday in the Park"(continued)

Bridge

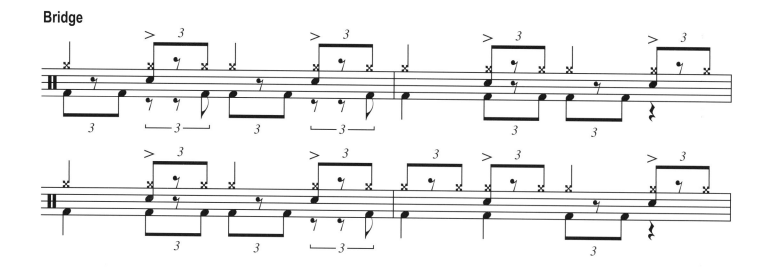

Ex 27 - Danny and Peter inject a dose of syncopation into the song's outro by displacing accents inside of the groove. (3:33)

Danny's Thoughts on "SATURDAY IN THE PARK"

I knew this song was special from the very first time that I heard it. Although Robert Lamm was brought up in Chicago he was born in Brooklyn. He's a New York boy, and this song has got that New York in the summer vibe. I love the lyrical message of the song too, it has a wonderful message about humanity. And outside of all of that, it's just a fun song. If you heard that drum part alone, you'd wonder what was going on. But when you hear it with the song, it makes perfect sense.

When I was growing up I (and the rest of the band) listened to The Rascals. Dino Danelli was sort of an "alternative" to Ringo for me. He had a ton of flair behind the drums. He played traditional grip, he flipped and twirled his sticks a lot, he had a great shuffle… I remember seeing them on the Ed Sullivan show, so when I created that drum part, I remember thinking that this is my tribute to Dino Danelli.

Peter's basslines are really the key to learning and playing that drum part. We were really locked in on that tune. Peter played very lyrical bass line, like McCartney does; But Peter stretched them out more, in my opinion he's a really under-rated bassist.

"Goodbye"- *Chicago V*

Ex 28 - Seraphine's expressive hi-hat work flows through the horn melody at the beginning of "Goodbye". The pedaled hi-hat steps add an interesting texture. (0:04)

"Goodbye"(continued)

Ex 29 - The song changes to 7/4 time going into the verse. Danny plays a straight 8th bossa nova groove that gels perfectly with the bass and guitar parts. (1:08)

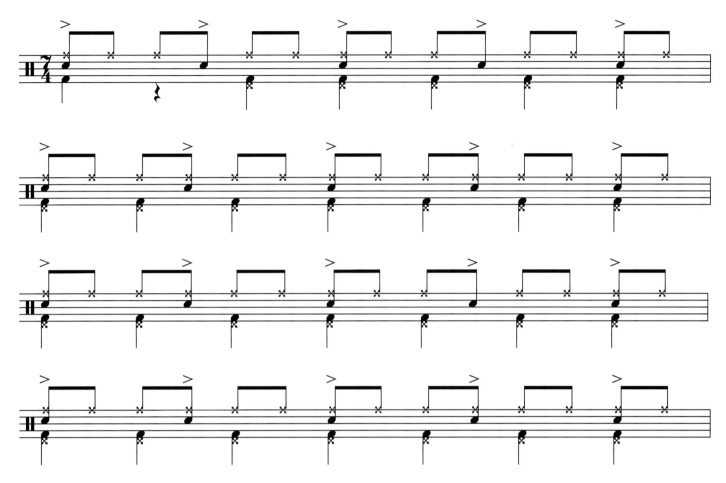

Ex 30 - When the main horn melody returns after the solo section, Seraphine swings hard and plays exciting fill phrases that elevate the action. (2:50)

"Goodbye" (continued)

Ex 31 - Danny plays a fill that brings the band into a new tempo after a big fermata. The drums and bass play an intricate 16th note funk groove that supports the big horn accents before the chorus vocals come in. (3:26)

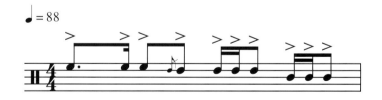

Chorus

Danny's Thoughts on "GOODBYE"

This is one of the times that I could really play authentic bebop style of swing in Chicago, I was really able to fuse bebop and rock on this tune. "Goodbye" epitomizes the fusing of those two approaches to timekeeping, there are some time changes too.

Chicago was spending a lot of time in NYC at the Village Vanguard, and I was studying with Papa Joe Jones around this time. "Goodbye" optimized what I learned from Papa Joe Jones and from listening to Elvin Jones. This track also has a strong 3/4 Art Blakey Jazz Messenger vibe too

However, the new Bossa Nova music was everywhere as well. I had come up doing gigs where you had to play many different styles of music, and Bossa Nova music like Stan Getz, Astrud Gilberto, and Jobim was one of the styles that

you just had to play. But it would sometimes come off sounding a little stiff. So when it came time to play the 7/4 sections in this tune, I suggested we play the Bossa Nova because it really complimented the lead vocal. The Rock Bossa feel translated really well to 7/4, and solved the problem of going from pure swing to the straight 7/4 section.

MD: Was the Bossa influence what led to adding percussionist to the band?

Danny: When I moved to California I became good friends with Sergio Mendes, we lived in the same town. We had a jam session at his house once, and I got to play with his percussionists Laudir de Oliviera and Paulinho DaCosta. Laudir and I just clicked. We already had a Latin vibe going on in the band already, so I thought that it was a very natural

thing to bring Laudir into Chicago. He really enhanced the music.

MD: Did you two guys arrange your parts as far as who would play what, and when to leave space for each other, or was it instinctual?

Danny: No we talked about it. We would make sure that patterns that we were playing together meshed, we would make sure that we weren't stepping on each other's parts. Sometimes I would ask him not to play congas on certain songs. Sometimes conga just doesn't fit into a tune, but many conga players force a conga part into the groove. Laudir was a great all-around percussionist, not just a conga player. He was terrific at hearing what tunes didn't need percussion and not playing anything if it wasn't needed.

"Another Rainy Day in New York City"- *Chicago X*

Ex 32 - "Another Rainy Day In New York City" is a song that brings out the Latin side of Danny's playing. The intro groove has a relaxed Brazillian-inspired feel with a samba foot pattern and a tom accent on the "and" of beat three. (0:00)

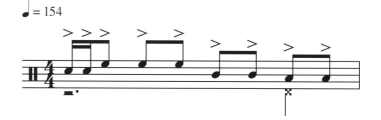

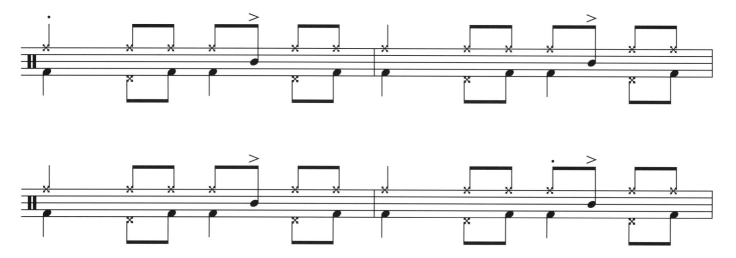

Ex 33 - This big fill rolls down all of the toms into the first chorus. (0:45)

Chorus

Ex 34 - He expands the pattern in the outro by bringing in additional tom and snare accents. (2:15)

Danny's Thoughts on "ANOTHER RAINY DAY IN NYC"

We were in New York City a lot back in those days, and during one stretch it seemed like it rained every day. That's a tasteful drum part that I am very proud of. I think it's a nice fusion of latin and rock. I never really studied latin music, but Bob Tilles had me playing some latin patterns, and began to play those patterns pretty instinctually. That's a nice song.

MD: How involved did you get with songwriting?

Danny: The first thing song I wrote was "Lowdown" from Chicago III. I didn't write again until I started writing for Chicago XI, and after I started writing I was always pretty involved. We were all usually involved in developing the songs. Robert Lamm was especially good at bringing in tunes and giving you a framework, but he would leave a lot of space for us to develop the song, and he let everyone do their own thing within the framework of the song.

On Chicago XI I had developed a strong relationship with keyboardist David "Hawk" Wolinsky. He was in a band called Madura and he was in Rufus. We wrote a lot of songs together where I wrote the lyrics and he wrote the melody and the chords. He's a brilliant musician and composer.

Danny's Thoughts on
"BALLET FOR A GIRL FROM BUCHANNON"

This is the entire multi-movement piece that contained "Make Me Smile" and "Color My World," and were included in the suite as separate movements. This definitely showcases the high level of musicianship and ground-breaking prowess of the band and my drumming. Everything is in there: Classical, R&B, Jazz, Rock… everything!

While we were touring for the first record, we had a few days off in Atlanta, and Jimmy Pankow had written this big suite for his girlfriend, so we learned and recorded it in separate sections, and then our producer pieced it together for the record. But then we had to learn it.

MD: How did you learn and remember the whole suite?

Danny: No tricks there, you just learn it. You read it off of the charts until you can put the charts away, and you play it a lot. But I don't care what anyone says, when you are reading a piece of music you aren't really playing it, you are READING it. When you are playing it, the music is coming from your heart and soul. In my opinion you aren't going to play as soulfully or as committed when you are reading. I'm not talking about session guys that don't have the luxury of time.

Continued on 92

"Ballet For A Girl In Buchannon" is an epic multi-movement piece that contains many different sections, including the well-known "Make Me Smile", "Colour My World", and the reprise "Now More Than Ever". Seraphine's well-rounded drumming leads the band through the arrangement with style and class.

"Make Me Smile"

Ex 35 - This classic two measure fill leads into the verse of "Make Me Smile." (0:38)

Ex 36 - Danny kicks the brass section through the first part of the chorus with an active pattern around the kit. He hooks up with the bass on a straight eighth groove near the end of the phrase and caps things off with a fast snare drum roll. (1:04)

"Make Me Smile" (continued)

Danny's Thoughts on "MAKE ME SMILE"

"Make Me Smile" is actually the beginning and the ending of a 12 minute suite called "Ballet for a Girl from Buchannon." The song was edited together after the entire suite had been recorded and released on our first album.

When I first heard this edited version I was driving in LA in my old Volkswagen Beetle with 150,00 miles on it. All of a sudden, I heard the DJ introduce "Make Me Smile" as the new Chicago single. I almost drove off the road because I had never heard it edited down. I stopped at a pay phone and called our manager and started cursing him out asking, "What are they doing to

our music by editing songs down. We never gave them permission to do that!" He stopped me short and said, "Danny, that song is being played on 75% of the AM radio stations in the country." I asked him, "Does that mean that I can go and buy a Mercedes? He said, "Yes." And the next day I went and bought my first Mercedes. That song really launched our career.

Thankfully, Clive Davis heard the song and thought it would be a hit single in a much shorter version, and he had the song edited down. I'm very proud to say that when they edited the song down (in the pre ProTools

days) the tempos matched perfectly. No one would ever have known that it was actually the beginning and the ending of a much longer song if they hadn't heard the longer suite on the record.

That's probably my most iconic drum part. That drum performance is my strong and obvious Buddy Rich/Gene Krupa influence fused with my Chicago R & B groove influences. The drum fills in the beginning, and the four bar fill at the end of the song are still a great source of pride for me. This song helped define me as a jazz/rock pioneer and as a musician.

"So Much to Say, So Much to Give"

Ex 37 - After a slight break in the action, Danny plays a triplet fill that sets the tempo for the 6/8 part of "So Much to Say, So Much to Give". He breaks the triplets up into groups of two and four to smoothly descend down the snare and toms. (0:11)

"West Virginia Fantasies"

Ex 38 - The drums and tambourine create a strong repetitive 3/4 groove that lays the groundwork for the instrumental movement "West Virginia Fantasies". (0:00)

Continued from 88

MD: When you guys recorded "Ballet for a Girl from Buchannon" were you reading or had you learned and memorized it by then?

Danny: I still had the charts next to me as a reference. I start the memorization process pretty quickly because (being dyslexic) I'm not a great reader.

MD: Were there charts involved for all Chicago tunes, or were tunes mostly learned by ear?

Danny: It happened both ways. But for the drums, my charts were usually chord charts with the hits written out, like traditional big band charts.

There is a bass drum part in "So Much To Say, So Much To Give" (from the suite) that everyone thinks that I used double bass drums on, but it's one foot. "West Virginia Fantasies" is my tribute to Jimmy Carl Black. Jimmy was so soulful and genuine, and he really liked Chicago and my playing, and that always made meant a lot. "To Be Free" is all about Buddy and Gene drum-wise.

"To Be Free"

Ex 39 - Seraphine lets the singles fly on a big extended fill in the intro of "To Be Free". (0:00)

"Now More Than Ever"

Ex 40 - The four measure solo in "Now More Than Ever" has become one of the most famous drum breaks in rock and roll history. Danny's style is exemplified here from the broken rhythms at the start, to the melodic toms in the middle, and finishing with a with a ripping snare drum roll. (0:44)

"Saturday in the Park" is a prime example of Seraphine's artistry in creating imaginative orchestrated parts. On the monster hit "Does Anybody Really Know What Time It Is?" Danny straddles an irresistible shuffle/ straight ...

... hybrid feel, while "Make Me Smile" opens with a soul syncopation setup, then drives ahead with an irresistible to-the-edge pulse. And on the later pop hit "Feelin' Stronger Every Day," he lays down a clean, grooving mid-tempo pocket.

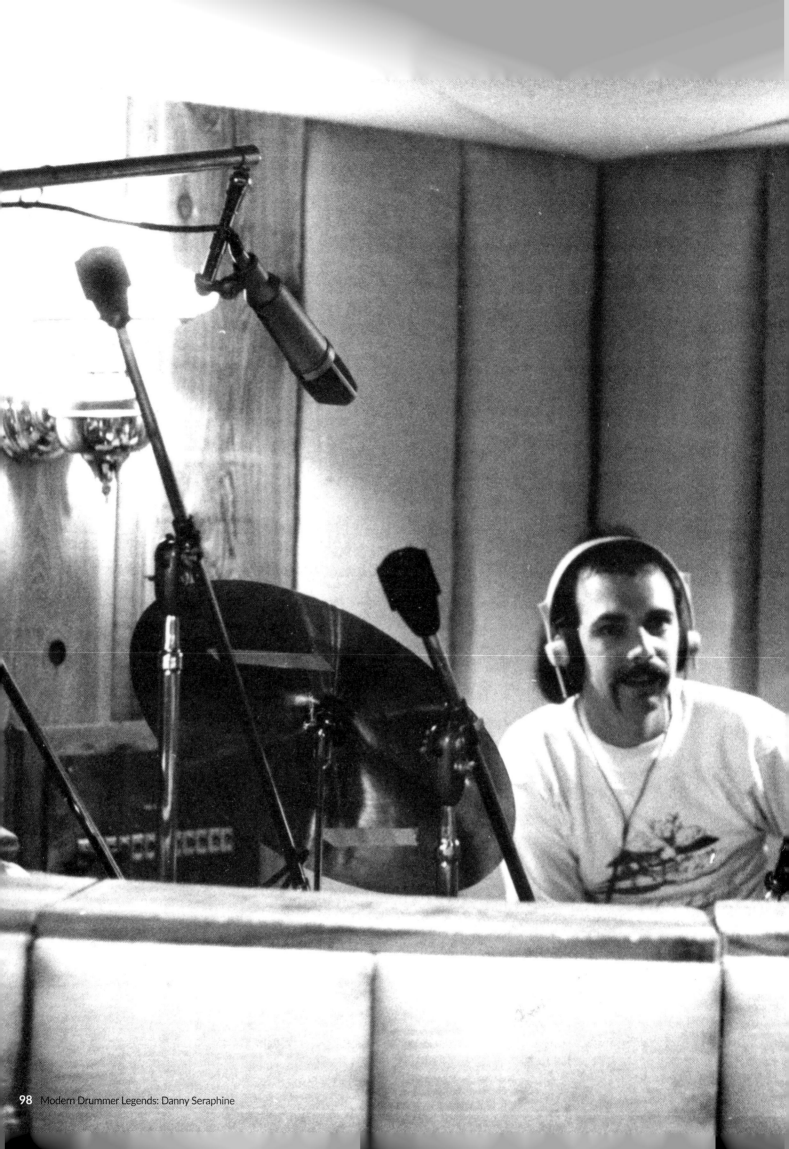